RETURN
VISIT

For the past six years Desmond Wilcox has worked for Wilcox Bulmer, his own production company, which has produced award-winning documentaries including *The Visit*. He was previously Head of BBC Television's General Features department. He is editor of *Explorers* (1975), he is also the author of *Americans* (1978) and, with his wife, *Kill the Chocolate Biscuit* (1981) and *Baby Love* (1985). He is married to Esther Rantzen, the presenter of *That's Life*. They live in London and have three children.

RETURN VISIT

DESMOND WILCOX

BBC BOOKS

Published by BBC Books,
a division of BBC Enterprises Limited,
Woodlands, 80 Wood Lane, London W12 0TT
First published 1991
© Desmond Wilcox 1991
ISBN 0 563 36052 6
Set in $11\frac{1}{2}$ on $13\frac{1}{2}$ pt Sabon
Printed and bound in Great Britain by
Butler & Tanner Ltd, Frome and London
Cover printed by R. Clay & Co, Norwich

CONTENTS

DEDICATION

To all the people of *The Visit* stories, both those mentioned
in this book – and those for whom there has been no space
here. Without them it couldn't have happened.
Without my family I couldn't have done it.

INTRODUCTION:
HOW *THE VISIT* BEGAN

The idea for *The Visit* series arose from a story I read in *The Guardian*, some ten years ago, when I was flying up to Edinburgh to take part in the television festival. The mother of a twelve-year-old spastic girl described the agonising decision she and her husband had come to, to put their child into care. She went on to write clearly and so precisely, that it made me weep when I read her article, of the weekly visit she now made to the child, the fifty-mile journey each way, the clumsy and inadequate 'saving up' of a week's emotions and affections. She wrote articulately and poignantly about her feelings of guilt, almost made worse by the realisation that her daughter was happy in the home, and loved, and well cared for. For the minutes it took to read the article I became part of an excoriating weekly experience in that loving mother's life. Her real purpose had been to draw attention to the need for more such homes, so that the difficulties of a long journey to visit a loved one (particularly for parents without a car) could be softened. If I was exhausted and moved by just reading it, how much more might she be, living it? But her article had taught me something of the strains, and the rewards, of a life I didn't know – and I was the better for it. And I had learned that a journey, a visit, is very often precisely the kind of action we take most for granted – yet it can illustrate, encapsulate, or just draw attention to the condition of other people, in a way that no comprehensive survey, no television dissertation or great debate could ever achieve.

At a party later that evening, to celebrate the success of Granada's *Jewel in the Crown*, I met the Controller of Television for BBC Scotland, Pat Chalmers, gazing with some cynicism at the festivities (the production had cost a fortune, and all television executives, yearning for large programme budgets, are jealous of others who have them).

'Are you really a freelance now?' he growled at me. I had, only the year before, given up my job as Head of General Features in BBC Television in London, in order to return to programme-making. 'You'd better believe it, or I may starve,' I told him.

'Let's have lunch soon and talk about it – I've talent up here, but I need an older hand to show them the way. Think of it as a kind of staff training exercise and if turns into more than that, then so be it,' he said.

It was in fact a completely normal exchange for this man, typically Aberdonian, gritty but perceptive. And lunch was always one of his favourite ways of doing business. We arranged to meet later next week in London and, before we turned back to the business of congratulating the opposition, he added: 'I don't suppose you'd want to work in Scotland, would you?' I was in Edinburgh from choice, I found Glasgow one of the most exciting and enjoyable cities in the world. It was also the home of documentary making (in the shape of John Grierson) and I would give much to have been born with Mac in front of my name and the right to call that country mine. I told him so. He grinned – and said 'Aye, you'll do.' Ten years later my family point out that I seldom use the word 'yes' myself, a permanent record of my time there.

We agreed to have lunch a week or so later, but before then I found myself talking with my wife's uncle, a distinguished chest consultant who had worked in some of the pioneering TB clinics, in the days when that disease was rampant. Patients were always there for long periods, the clinics were often situated far from their homes, visits by relatives were usually not encouraged more frequently than about once a month. And visiting day was, for the staff, a day to be dreaded. They always knew that the patients would be worse when it was over. The tension, the anticipation was so great that the day could only be a disappointment and would knock back their progress. And yet, said my uncle-in-law, it was a time when one learned so much more about a patient, gained the extra information that would help the staff improve his lot, under-stand his condition the better. 'Yes,' he said. 'The visit was often disturbing – but we always learned from it.'

When, eventually, I met Pat Chalmers in London, he brought along the acting Head of Television Features for BBC Scotland, Neil Fraser. Over lunch I told them of my idea: a series of films, each would follow a person on a journey, towards a goal, confronting a challenge. The stories would be entirely personal, not at all 'balanced' in the way that the BBC always thought necessary at the time, not comprehensive television surveys of problem areas, with every opinion qualified by another view.

The films would have a beginning, we would know where to start. But we could only guess where we might be in the middle and would be most unlikely ever to know how they would end. A dangerous exercise in BBC terms – tantamount to gambling. In this area of documentary-making, I told them, I felt myself to be a professional gambler – a good bet. The stories would always, without fail, follow a chronological narrative style – no second guessing in commentary, no unfair intercutting of views so that we could make ourselves seem wiser than we deserved. And the people, the people at the centre of these stories, would have to be given a share in the programme-making decisions. That was almost unprecedented within the BBC at that time. But these people, I said, would be allowing *us* to learn from *their* experiences – and even if they themselves might also learn from telling their own story, they still needed the assurance of responsible control over what they had volunteered to do. It was agreed.

Only weeks later we were working in Glasgow. Three of us: not the smallest documentary team ever but certainly nearly so. We moved, from cupboard, to Portakabin, to attic, to basement gloom, about every four months. I suspect that, as far as BBC book-keeping went, we didn't officially exist. We consisted of an ex-film editor, Alex McCall; a production assistant, Jan Riddell, and me. For the first series we were loaned the services of the talented Jackie Rowley, now a reporter, but then making one of her first full-length films, and

Brian Barr, a seasoned news producer, seconded from Current Affairs. We all determined to start by making the film of the story I had read in *The Guardian*.

I traced the writer and telephoned her. She burst into tears. 'I would love nothing more, how wonderful it would be.' There was a long silence before she added: 'But my beautiful, lovely daughter died only last month.'

She was a wonderful woman, she perceived immediately what we hoped to achieve and helped us, through The Spastics Society, and then through Mencap, to find another, similar case – parents who were actually at that moment about to make the decision to put their daughter into a home – and start the tortured, self-castigating process of weekly visits. The film, directed by Jackie Rowley, was called 'Seeing Jemima'.

Brian Barr had discovered, through a local newspaper-clipping, the story of a Yorkshire coal-miner who had never known his mother and now, through a fluke had found her, in a pit village outside Edinburgh. So far, there had been phone calls and now there was about to be the first visit – she was making the journey to meet the son she'd been forced to give away as a baby; he was preparing his wife and children for the granny they didn't know they had. That became 'Mother for Malcolm'.

And Alex McCall wanted us to tell, on television, the story that had been told so far only in the Glasgow papers but in which the central characters had steadfastly refused to be filmed, because they had been so horrified by sensational mis-reporting in some papers. The people were in America, where I was about to take my family on holiday. That is how I came to spend two days of that holiday on the phone, talking to one of the most remarkable women I've ever met, and her brilliant and compassionate husband. The result was not one but two films, in that first series – 'The Boy David' and 'Marjorie's Quest'. It was the most outstanding story I've ever been allowed to tell. It was to win the hearts of the nation – and the top international documentary award.

We were hardly just a training exercise any more. Now we had achieved the status of a network documentary series on

BBC 1. But we had done it, through the talent of our team, the great support of Features and mostly, and in the end, only, because the people of *The Visit* also believed in our purpose.

Now, years on, we are no longer part of BBC Scotland, but part of the Independent sector, making the films for the BBC from our own company in London. I loved working in Scotland and didn't want to leave, but the management has changed and the present head of Television wanted to do other things, things more Scottish, with his air time. Fortunately the BBC continues to encourage us to make *The Visit* series – and we will. The stories are still there to be told, many of them. And these days people contact us with ideas and the names of people they think we should meet.

I miss Glasgow, friends and colleagues, like the two Aileens who were eventually to join our team as production assistant and production secretary. But Alex McCall commutes and Jan Riddell, now the assistant producer, has moved south. So the original three of us are still together, determined, while we are able and allowed to, to go on telling stories for television – stories of *The Visit*.

CHAPTER ONE

WHY RETURN?

In nearly nine years there have been more than forty stories, forty journeys, forty groups of people – travelling through a situation, confronting a dilemma, locked into circumstances and emotions beyond the experience of most of us: the people of *The Visit*. And for part of that time we have travelled with them, shared their experience and then shared it further with a television audience, millions of other families watching, sympathising, perhaps learning: not entertainment but still compelling; not education but nevertheless a lesson for all of us.

But the lesson we on *The Visit* team didn't seek to learn was about ourselves. We filmed our stories always with the emphasis on the partnership, not just the participation of our subjects. We showed the finished product first to those who were its central characters, we invited comment and, if needed, made adjustment. This offer of co-operation was not just a cosmetic gesture (not unheard of in television programme-making), but a genuine desire to get things right, to avoid doing harm by broadcasting material which perhaps – on later reflection – would be too painful, or likely to cause a damaging reaction, particularly the morning after as many as ten million people had seen it the night before.

We became very close to all of the people in our *Visit* films, and still stay in touch with most of them. But do we really know what happened to them after we had packed our equipment and left? Had our presence, at the time, made the situation they faced seem artificial? Were things easier or more difficult to deal with in the long term?

What happens when we take the spotlight off their problem? Take the sympathetic listening ear away, remove the busy and cheerful distractions of a team of experts – needing coffee, wanting to listen, offering professional understanding – and is life flat, are people let down and regretful when we have all gone?

It is of course a dangerous and introspective thing to ask oneself. Is it self-justification, morbid introspection? Is it the rationalisation which comes from leaving behind people who will still have to struggle every day to cope with the kind of lives you almost daren't wonder if you, personally, could handle? Is it the guilt of the person who observes a famine – and returns to a hotel for dinner? The counsellor who offers advice, hears someone else's pain, and then moves on to the next case?

But a documentary film cannot be, has no time to be – unless it is overwhelmingly indulgent – a film about the making of the film. It is, and should be, quite simply the telling of a story, someone else's story. In telling that story, the person describing the events, remembering the emotions, thinking – perhaps for the first time – about their own reactions and responses, may go through a process of cathartic release, rid themselves of the tension that comes from 'bottling up' emotions. They may, and frequently they do, find the words to say for the first time what has always before been the unspeakable thought: 'I wish he had not been born.' 'I do not wish to be brave, I want to cry, I want to surrender, let go.' 'Caring for someone who needs total devotion may improve your chances with God but it damages the fabric of your marriage to a man.'

And: 'I thought I believed in God but the more I see of the misery he has allowed, the more I think he can't be much of a God.'

That last from a heroine, Pat Kerr, British Airways stewardess and the woman who mobilised her colleagues, and the viewing public, around the work of a desperately struggling orphanage in Dhaka, Bangladesh.

But after ... after they've voiced those unspeakable thoughts, is there regret, recrimination, a sense of having shattered, beyond repair, something that should have been kept intact and private? On this machine, on which I write, I can erase a thought, cancel a phrase, even go back and conceal again, a truth that perhaps I should not have revealed, by the simple expedient of pressing a key marked 'delete'. But once spoken in front of witnesses, fixed and recorded on film and sound tape, broadcast to millions, there is no going back. Life, documentary life at any rate, has no 'delete' key.

But all this is miserable, masochistic and not altogether fair to film-makers. Most people feel better, benefit from speaking about their struggle, both with life and self. As with a stranger on a train, it even works out that one's difficulties are sometimes carried away by the person who listened, lifted from one's shoulders. And much real and lasting good has followed in the wake of *The Visit* stories. Charities have sprung into existence and prosper still. Self-help groups have emerged to share experiences and improve the individual lot because of it. In hospital committees, in government departments, changes have taken place. Not huge, not world-shattering, except that they are for those most in need of recognition or help.

But there is, also, the aspect of documentary filming that the viewer never sees – has no need to see – because there is not time on the screen and because it would be too personal and subjective, not part of the process of story-telling. There is a constant struggle to find enough money to make a film; there are fights with bosses. (One of ours believed that if you had your laundry done by the hotel where you were staying, then you were squandering licence-payers' money. You should carry at least fifteen spare shirts, he maintained, then confessed that even he didn't own that number.) There are the exhausting arguments with broadcasting rule-book bureaucrats, hassles with 'job's worth' officials, enforcing rules and union procedures, wherever you are and wherever you travel. I once had a stand-up row with a cameraman, in the middle of the jungle, on the bank of the Amazon, just before boarding two huge dug-out canoes, when he told me that the BBC rules made it clear that we should have brought out from Britain standard issue life-jackets.

We had just flown across the Andes in a light, unpressurised plane, barely able to carry us, our equipment and food supplies.

In a rage I managed to roar at him: 'I shouldn't worry about the absence of life-jackets. If you fall in, the piranha fish will strip you to the bone long before you reach the bank.' In fact, we were at least a thousand miles from any piranha fish – but it all serves to illustrate what is the main, time-consuming activity behind the scenes on a documentary.

There are also the many discussions behind the scenes about the people we are filming, what we might reasonably ask to be allowed to film, how best to illustrate their situation, what we can do to help, without taking over and interfering: talks in camera cars, hotel rooms – rather like a social work team, quietly assessing the best way ahead.

But there is another problem: what if you find you don't actually like the person you've come to make the centre of a film? How do you conceal your reaction to greed, vanity, insensitivity? You may have to, not for hypocritical reasons but because there is still a worthwhile story to be told. One of our heroes hated blacks, Jews, homosexuals and certainly didn't respect women. I sat next to him at dinner every night for weeks, heard his hateful opinions scores of times over a period of years. And yet his personal example has inspired hundreds of disabled people, particularly children; his achievement has brought a splendid charity into being. I have found, over the years, that those who are admirable are not always likable – but there is no rule that says they should be. (I have met and interviewed a number of men and women who have won the highest honours for gallantry and many of them, one or two of the soldiers in particular, have been arrogant, not always intelligent and certainly unimaginative people who have reacted frequently from rage, or instinct.) Most truly admirable heroes, in my view, are the people who fear what they're doing, who know the weariness that is almost invariably a concomitant of goodness – and still go on with it. But admiration isn't guaranteed. So, like a lawyer or a social worker, it is always possible to take refuge in the professional manner, the formula of television film-making. But for *The Visit* films this doesn't really work. To make the visit you have to be close to your subject.

It explains perhaps – but does not, of course, forgive – why on one occasion I blew it. It was during the filming of *The Marriage* series, a spin-off from *The Visit* and directed by John Pettman, in which we followed a young Welsh couple from just before their wedding day up to their first anniversary. I had already warned my own team never to quarrel with the 'customers' when they became difficult, even petulant. But on the last day of filming I was the one who lost his cool. That day, at the end of more than twelve months, I found our hero and his friends sabotaging the film director's car – we were about to drive back to London in it – as a great joke. I lost restraint – and went on at length, unpardonably, to our young groom, star of the series. I only fully realised what damage I had done when our electrician, who had been standing near, said: 'You didn't repeat yourself once, Desi.'

And Alex McCall once rejoined our dinner table to whisper to me that he had just lost his temper with P.C. Philip Olds, whose heroic determination to walk although he was paralysed by a gunman's bullet was the subject of our film. Alex, stung to rage, had swung Philip's wheelchair against the tiled wall of the Gents, trying to knock some sense into Philip – after watching him behave insufferably to his fiancée.

Unforgivable lapses – perhaps understandable. Certainly the stories can now be retold because the people involved were the first to understand that the pressure also rubs off on the production team.

But, probably most important of all, the reason for making a return visit is quite simply just to find out how people have been doing, since we last heard or saw them. What is David like now? How has Connie continued to recover from that terrible world of coma? How are the young couple of *The Marriage*? Is the unforgettable young man, dying of AIDS in San Francisco, but still trying to help others, still alive? And, for some stories, we have been back once, or twice, with the film camera, and they have been the most applauded by the public. That is proof enough that telling the story in the first place was justified. 'Tell me more' always means it was good to tell it in the beginning.

So, this is more, and a little of what wasn't said then; a view behind the scenes as well as a reminder of what you saw at the time, and an update rather than a remake, certainly not the documentary equivalent of *Rambo Six*. These chapters can't be the reworking of an old story – *The Visit* stories didn't stop when we finished filming, people's lives have gone on and their stories can continue to be of interest and value to those of us who learned from them to start with.

CHAPTER TWO

CONNIE – THE GIRL IN COMA

Connie's is the only *Visit* story that didn't start with a person, but with an idea. I had met, after one of my wife's *That's Life* programmes, an impressive man, Reg Talbot, the National Director of Headway, the charity which fights for head-injured people. He had been helping *That's Life* with an astonishing case of obduracy between county councils, which was costing a girl desperately in need of treatment the opportunity she needed. After the broadcast, which later prodded bureaucracy into action, we talked of the mythology that surrounds head injuries – the mythology that we on television are responsible for perpetrating.

If cowboys are hit over the head with a gun butt or a chair, if Bond is knocked out (for a few minutes) with a blow from an iron bar, if Indiana Jones is buried by a rock fall, or hammered by a prize fighter, within minutes they shake their heads and carry on as normal.

In real life you would be lucky to live, and you would certainly be damaged, changed and disabled, for the rest of your life, by any one of the blows the stuntmen pretend to take for our heroes. And what of coma, that long dark sleep in another world still not properly understood by doctors or scientists. Do Sleeping Beauties wake, with a kiss, and return, exactly as before, to the life they left?

Coma is a condition that more people go through than most of us realise – and from which they never return the same. The doctors, the surgeons and the physiotherapists, the nurses and the speech therapists, who work with such dedication in this area of medicine, know that they have not only to fight to recover the patient, they have to teach the relatives to 'unlearn' all that they thought they knew about head injuries.

Some people never come out of coma, very few. Some stay in coma for too long, longer usually means more damage. Ten thousand people a year go into coma, their lives as shattered as their skulls. For those who come back from that world of darkness, where life hangs in precarious balance, they bring no memory of their time in limbo – and they rejoin us, changed for ever. To follow such a case, to share with a family that dreadful dark learning, would seem almost too heavy, too intrusive. But Reg Talbot pointed out that the patient is already in intensive care, wired to machines, plugged into life support. Intensive care units are not soulful places of peace and rest. They are high-tech rooms buzzing with electronic life-saving equipment. The relative, a wife, husband or parent, is usually desperately in need of some distraction from the impossible task of sitting by a living corpse, holding hands with someone who has already left, urging a loved one to return from the edge of the final shadowland. The relatives, in these cases, are learning and – through a film – so could we.

We met Graham Teasdale, the consultant neuro-surgeon, at Southern General Hospital, Glasgow. He's a Yorkshireman, saving lives in a city which has the highest number of head injuries in the country. They used to call it the Saturday Night Syndrome. You know, 'when I've had a couple of drinks on a Saturday (hic), Glasgow belongs to me.' But usually the truth is that the singer belongs in the emergency operating theatre, having stepped in front of a car or bus, and he's lucky if his life belongs to him. And, if it does, then it is because of skills in Glasgow neuro-surgical units, like that of the Southern General.

Graham Teasdale agreed that the purpose of the film was good, even needed. But how to go about it? We met the rest of his team and other medical staff. We all agreed how we should behave, what we should film. We didn't know who.

Graham Teasdale knew that it was impossible to predict, with great accuracy, what sort of coma, what depth of coma, a new patient was in. Complete, vegetative coma would give the public the wrong idea, it was the most dramatic in one sense and the least frequent in reality. So, we would wait, wait to hear if a patient arrived, if the family were prepared to be filmed, if the hospital thought it wise, if everyone agreed. I was not at all sure that we had much chance of making this important film and we turned the attention of our research to other things. Penny Hallowes, our researcher on this project, went on visiting the experts, making sure that they knew we were waiting ... and waiting.

The phone call came two days after Christmas. The *Visit* team were scattered, in their homes, digesting turkey with their families. But Graham Teasdale had been true to his promise. And suddenly, tragically, *The Visit* no longer had an idea, we had a person – Connie.

Connie Taylor, just eleven years old, had been spending her Christmas money, with her sisters, when she ran out in front of a bus, on the dual carriageway, only yards from her home. An overtaking taxi struck her. The driver was not to blame: he had no chance to see her, barely time to brake before his bumper threw her into the road, fracturing ribs, puncturing her lung – and shattering her skull. They can mend the skull, the casing for that most fragile of all human mechanisms, the brain, but saving the life of a little girl, whose brain has been pounded like a computer thrown from a height, is too frequently beyond the skills of even the best surgeons. When Graham Teasdale was called to see Connie she had been moved to his hospital from the emergency ward to which the ambulance had first delivered her. It was clear that she was going to need emergency brain surgery. And from that moment the whole family were towed along in the tyrannical slow motion of personal tragedy, as the people who deal professionally with death and disaster took over. Doreen Taylor, Connie's mother, aching for the daughter who might be dying, was by then an impotent spectator at the centre of her own family drama.

They operated for blood clots under the skull – twice. The punctured lung was nearly as life-threatening, and they fought to repair that damage. After more than six hours in the operating theatre, they were able to transfer her to an intensive care ward – on a ventilator, wired to machines, watched constantly. Doreen had travelled with her in the ambulance and then Connie had been semi-conscious, moaning, murmuring – at least (it seemed to Doreen) still alive, with a chance to win through. Now, Connie was in coma: still, white, apparently lifeless.

Coma comes from the classical Greek word for 'deep sleep' and in ancient times it was believed that the moon goddess Diana watched over the affairs of one who slept so soundly. Scientists still don't understand the process; doctors can only make forecasts, based on experience, but still not much more scientific than expert guesswork. The body may have been mended, patched, stitched and soothed – but what of the mind? What chance was there that Graham Teasdale could mend her mind? Connie had gone to a place filled with discordant echoes and broken memories, a twilight world, from which she might return, but only might. And, if she did, she would be changed. The old Connie would never return.

For Doreen, half-sitting, half-crouched by Connie's side in the intensive care ward, this was just the beginning of an agonisingly slow process. All the staff knew what was ahead, how long, how painful and exhausting. We knew too – they had told us – but there was no way we could help, little we could offer. Doreen was, in many ways, alone, needing to draw on her own strength and emotional resources to cope with the present, even to begin to consider the future. She has four children, Connie is the youngest. One minute she was alive – the next, not dead but not truly alive, beyond reach – in limbo.

'What sign?' Doreen asked the staff, and us. 'What sign can I look for?' And there is no immediate answer in those early hours of coma, no direction you can give a mother praying for her child to come back. And back from where? The experts told her to go on trying, her heart told her to keep on hoping. She told us she wanted, positively wanted, to be part of a *Visit* documentary. Her reason? The place where Connie was knocked down is a notorious danger spot on a busy dual carriageway. Many times parents and concerned local people have demanded a zebra crossing on this fast, straight piece of road. Now, reasoned Doreen, they may listen. Even if they didn't it was important, she felt, to drive home to parents and children the lessons of road safety, the road crossing drill they're all supposed to know by heart and – with lethal consequences – sometimes forget when their young spirits are high and careless.

I knew that, whatever happened, Doreen was going to be a person I would remember all my life, and always admire. She is a single parent – her husband left years before – struggling with pride, without complaint, to support and bring up well her loved and beautiful family. Life for her was already a tiring and difficult battle with the demands of a job, she's a receptionist for the local health authority, and the even more draining demands of a healthy family of four children.

In the past caring for coma patients was regarded as looking after the living dead, a natural reaction to the complete absence of response or life. But Doreen, taking time off work, spent hours chafing Connie's hands, talking to her, nudging at her memory with stories of friends from school, tales of what was going on at home, willing her, with every fibre of her being, to show some flicker, some tiny sign. Nothing. The night nurse in the intensive care ward was Mr Murray. He saw what was happening, he's a good and experienced nurse.

'Don't be frightened,' he told Doreen. 'Don't be frightened at all. You cuddle her, don't be frightened of all the tubes and wires and machines – you just talk to her, hug her, give her a kiss. Let us worry about the plastic and the machines.'

Connie stayed in coma for weeks. Doreen, back at work as the bread-winner, journeyed twice a day right across Glasgow to spend hours by her bed. Her school friends made cassette recordings, sending messages to Connie from the classroom where her desk stayed poignantly empty. From the hospital bedside table, the cassette player boomed the young voices, shouting their messages of love – and there was no response. The physiotherapists, unbelievably patient and skilful, worked every day with Connie – and they might as well have been manipulating an anaesthetised patient. Connie's favourite recording star is Shakin' Stevens, they played his music to her – and her face remained white and immobile. Doreen got in touch with him – and he travelled to Glasgow to visit Connie. He's a kind and generous man who has already done similar things for other injured and damaged children. He is, himself, a family man and knows what it might feel like to be a parent in a case like this. By Connie's bed, with the nurses crowded at the window to peer at this famous and surprisingly self-effacing star, he stayed for an hour and talked to Connie. Nobody will ever really know if her vague twitching at that time was just part of the restless healing process going on in her head, or a response to her hero. He left cassettes, kissed her and promised to stay in touch. And he did.

By now Connie's eyes were open but sightless, unseeing and unrevealing. All of us were learning a great deal about head injuries. Connie's hand was bent and twisted, her foot frozen and curled up, all as a result of her head injury. And it is also the whole family that can be injured in a case like this. Doreen had taken as much time off as the health authority rules permit. Any more time and she'd have had to take unpaid leave, go on the dole. Dr John Brydon the head of community medicine for Greater Glasgow was one of the medical bosses who had approved of our making this extended documentary in the first place. His task is to see that the right kind of support is made available, not only to the victim of a head injury, but to the family. And yet when we interviewed him about his role, he learned for the first time that Connie's mother worked for his own authority; indeed, he met her at least twice a week. He is a hard-working and dedicated man, determined to set up worth-while support services for families like Doreen's. He was appalled to discover that the child he knew we had been filming was the daughter of one of the health authority's staff.

'I feel ghastly about it,' he told us. 'Very guilty – I know her mother and there may have been something I could have done, sooner, to help her. It just proves how we must work to see that people aren't left without help or understanding in cases like this.'

It went on for weeks – and weeks. Connie (who had long flowing hair up until the accident) moved her shaven head from side to side, the scars of brain surgery fresh and raw. She opened her eyes, gazed unseeingly around her. She made noises, the almost mewling noises of a small baby, irritated by light or noise – puzzled and frightened by the world she was facing. Sometimes, sometimes only, she appeared to recognise her mother's voice, respond to the pressure of her mother's hand over hers. But she was still in coma.

Graham Teasdale told us: 'The coma is lighter now but she is still there, not yet out. It's easy to deceive oneself and believe that it's all about to be over. It's not: there's a very long way to go – and the people who have to be made to understand that are the patient's family. They also have to understand that Connie won't be the same when she does come out of coma; not just different for a while, but changed for all time. There will be physical damage to repair and work on, the paralysed hand and twisted foot, but there will also be the lack of memory, the absence of speech, the need to learn everything, I mean everything, again. There are months and months of painful treatments and physiotherapy, and speech therapy and learning and learning and learning, ahead of her. A long depressing grind. There is no other way.

'But', he went on, 'she is emerging from coma and the predictions are good, perhaps even as much as a seventy-five per cent recovery.' But for all of us that so-called good news was a shock. Only seventy-five per cent. Like most people, weaned on stories of the Sleeping Beauty, wakened with a kiss, emerging gently and smilingly back into the world unchanged by her long deep absence from it, we, and everybody else, thought recovery might be more complete, more magic. Life isn't like that.

Doreen took it well, she more than us had come to understand what was ahead. Ten weeks after the accident she knew she'd get her daughter back, not yet, not completely. The old Connie would never return.

In the Knockburn primary school, Connie's friends grew, advanced and progressed. In the Southern General hospital time dragged in a drawn-out version of those cricketing action replays on television, nearly at a standstill, agonisingly slow. On the notice-board in the main corridor of Connie's school they had kept the handiwork of her classmates, prepared just before the Christmas holiday, the holiday in which time stood still for Connie. On one of our filming days, while waiting for the crew to pack up their equipment, I spotted in the centre of the board, a poem, written by Connie. I motioned to Alex McCall to stop the crew leaving. Minutes later the camera was set up and filming Connie's poem, written only ten days before Connie herself became frozen in time:

> **The snow is melting on our hands,**
> **It looks like little freckles,**
> **It is raining,**
> **The snow is turning into slush,**
> **It looks like lots of swirley slimey snakes.**
> **I love snow.**
> **I wish it was here all the time.**

Eight weeks after the accident Connie was taken to the operating theatre again. This time to have the bone flap, that had been removed from her skull, replaced by surgery. For two months Connie's fragile, damaged brain had been protected only by skin over the area the size of a small saucer. But new born babies have the soft fontanelle in the centre of the head, a gentle, sensitive reminder of their fragility. And, in a way, Connie was new born – again. After ten weeks they tried an experiment – and let her go home for the weekend with her mother. She still had no speech, only excited baby noises; she couldn't walk without dragging her foot; her hand remained curled, the fingers stiff. Her delight as she reached the front door was obvious, her memory clearly a happy one. Her mother helped her through the door, with tears in her eyes. It was to this door, just three days after Christmas, that Connie was running – when she was struck, and changed, changed for ever. Connie had come back, but not the old Connie – this new Connie had many more miles to travel.

By now we had been filming, a day here, a day there, for nearly three months. Alex and I both knew that we already had enough material to fill a fifty-minute documentary, fill it tightly, too. But Connie hadn't even left hospital yet although she was expected to within a few weeks. When she did, then there was a mountain to climb, for Connie and Doreen. All the physiotherapy, the speech therapy, the comprehension testing, the whole range of healing and teaching that might have to go on for another year or more, would be based from home. It would test the resources of the Glasgow health authority. It would stretch to breaking point the human resources of Connie's family. It had to be filmed. To stop now would be like leaving a long-distance race half-way through, never to know the end. The hospital authorities agreed, so did Doreen. By now we had all become good friends – Doreen had even taken me to a wild social occasion, the Balornock Ladies Night, and I had escaped this high-voltage, and overpowering evening with my skin and reputation intact, just. But there was the problem of the BBC. Would they allow us to make two of our *Visit* programmes about one little girl's struggle to regain a place in the world?

I went to the Head of Television for BBC Scotland, Jim Hunter, with the proposition and found him not unsympathetic – but with certain reservations. He agreed that the two-part chronicle of Connie's fight would be good, even responsible television. He was suspicious that we would be making an easier life for ourselves, not properly earning our pay. However, we went on filming.

After thirteen weeks Connie came home for good. Penny Hallowes, who had patiently and tirelessly stayed in touch with every nurse, every doctor and every teacher on the case, was as tearful as the rest of us, while we filmed the homecoming that might never have happened. What we were creating on film, we began to realise, was more than just the story of courage, the chronicle of a family endeavour – it was a unique record of just what is really meant by the casual term 'head injury'. At meetings of the local Headway Association we saw, for the first time, how self-help groups like this are vital to the survival of the patients and their families. We saw, too, how much more support and finance they needed, more time from the already overworked experts. The dramatic image of brilliant brain surgeons, using daring and skill to bring people back from the brink of death in one swift event, became for us what it always has been, more the invention of Hollywood script writers or the fantasy of tabloid journalists.

At home Connie had wild swings of mood. She's a big, mature girl, almost it seemed too big for the baby treatment she craved. Doreen found her demands to sit on her lap and be cuddled, particularly in public, difficult to cope with. But gradually some speech was returning, some memory had come back, the process of teaching was unbelievably grinding. After a hundred repetitions Connie would say one word properly – only to have forgotten it completely by the morning. Connie regularly went back to the hospital for progress checks and tests. Doreen had been forced to take six months' leave of absence from her job – without pay. Life was hard in every way.

On one morning, also, there was a surprise for Connie. Shakin' Stevens, who true to his word had kept in touch, turned up at her door. We had been let in on the secret and Connie thought we were just there to do more 'ordinary' filming of her progress. Her face when she opened the front door of their council house, to find her hero on the step, was an image to treasure. Because we were filming we were able to share with viewers the shock and pleasure that registered on Connie's face. A very special moment was captured for millions. But does that mean the moment became, in retrospect, somehow less special? – Was broadcasting it perhaps a form of intrusion? Certainly, the kind of critics who sharpen their typewriter ribbons when they see *The Visit* in schedules, would leap to say so. They expect us to behave in that peculiarly British way and not show emotion in public or – even worse – watch someone else doing so. *The Visit* therefore goes down on both counts. And my response has always been – 'Rubbish!' In fact, such moments are always seen by the people most concerned (in this case Doreen and Connie) well before transmission and in good time to register doubt or objection if that is the reaction. But it isn't. Doreen is positively glad that we showed that – and other rather emotional moments – in the final film. She told me:

'It is true that you open up your home and your life, even your very private thoughts and feelings. But you don't feel that you're doing anything wrong, certainly I was never pressured by Penny or you or Alex or anybody on the team to behave in a way I wouldn't want to. And I don't regret it, I didn't have one pause about it after the films had transmitted – no second thoughts at all. Actually, I felt that I was sharing all my problems with other people – and I was also sharing the better moments. I think often of people who are going through situations like mine and I believe they might have been helped a bit just to know that they weren't alone, that someone else could go through it and come out still smiling. Doctors are cautious about committing themselves in so many ways that I somehow knew that by sharing the experiences I was going through I would be helping other people in the same situation – and that knowledge helped me too.'

The weary process dragged on. Connie had to learn, again, everything – speech, reading, writing – literally everything. At times it must have seemed to Doreen that she was always going to have a child who was a victim, almost mute, with no memory or capacity for retention. But the system tried, and often failed. And then Doreen, determined and almost seemingly inexhaustible, would push harder, to make it work. And Connie's teacher from before the accident, Miss Hendry, got together with the educational therapist. And Connie went on, a thousand times, saying b – b – b – or d – d – d –. And slowly she grew from a mental age of a few months, to a few years – even towards her real age of twelve. Neighbours sensed the strain of it all and organised a charity fun run. The Taylors were never well off but now they faced the problem of being really poor. Doreen had given up her job to be with Connie full-time, they were all living on social security. Doreen is a proud woman who would never seek out charity for herself but she knew the neighbours' gesture had been a warm-hearted, Glaswegian effort, and that it would cause huge offence to refuse. They collected £700 – and gave it to her at a rather wild night in a local social club. Then, I saw Connie, smiling, dreamy-eyed with pleasure, dancing. So did her surgeon.

Graham Teasdale told me: 'She'll make it – that is a picture of a person coming back to life. Wonderful.'

The family went on day trips – to the seaside at Ayr. And some of the money raised by the neighbours went towards a package holiday in Spain. And, on one special weekend, they were sent tickets to a Shakin' Stevens concert in Edinburgh; transport was laid on – he had not forgotten the girl in coma. He even dedicated one of his songs to her, as she sat in a box almost rigid with excitement, blushing with a pulsing pleasure as he sang his latest single: 'I love you'. Connie may have failed to recover much of her previous memory but she was certainly laying down new memories to make any teenager envious.

A year, almost to the day, after her accident we went with her while she was assessed by the neuro-pyschologist, Ruth Gillman. A day rather like an eleven-plus examination – but this time Connie was being examined to see if she had qualified to re-enter the life she lost when the taxi hit her. And if she did – at what level, how much lower, might she qualify? The results were good, still a long way to go – but the Taylors were able at least to look towards the day when Connie would go back to her old school, perhaps two years below her old class. While her classmates reach forward for what they have yet to know, Connie must learn to reach backwards for what she has forgotten. Then, fourteen months after the accident, Connie did go back to school. She had asked about the accident, she clearly had no knowledge of it all, and had been told. She didn't know what a miracle she was and the day we all watched her walk through the school gates for the first time in nearly eighteen months, Doreen said: 'I tell her it's been a miracle – but I think she'll only realise it when she sees it all on television.

'She wants to see the films and I think it will help her enormously to do so. Even though she sometimes gets distressed and disturbed by me talking to her about it, when she asks me questions, I think this is one way she can fill in those empty places in her mind, the gaps of knowledge that still bother and hurt her. When I got her home from the hospital I was, at first, so relieved just to have her alive that I didn't really understand what was ahead of me – and her. The struggle has been the most exhausting thing I've ever been through. And the most worth-while,' she paused and added: 'You've got to understand that what I was left with wasn't the same wee girl I once had. It was like a stranger really – it was like starting all over again, with somebody else. Teaching her everything. It just wasn't Connie. I mean, when I think about it, the Connie I had just died that night.'

We were coming to the end of our filming, we had even watched, with our hearts in our mouths, while Connie rediscovered cycling, in the local park – weaving and wobbling between the early daffodils. Never had spring seemed so certain in its annual message of promises to come. We visited Graham Teasdale, who still saw Connie for regular check-ups, and will continue to do so for years. I asked him the kind of question no doctor or surgeon really likes; it involves personal speculation. But his experience and his understanding make him the kind of surgeon most likely to be able to answer it – and most likely to try. He told me:

'I feel she's a success. She will clearly never be the same girl again, this kind of injury, that length of time in coma and in hospital does change people, a lot. But I think that what we must point out is that looking back, in these circumstances, is wrong. I think everyone needs to think: "What's Connie like now and what is she going to do in the future with her new personality?" I think one of the best things you can observe is that she was obviously a nice little girl before and that's stayed the same. And I think that's helping her. Yes, I think she's a success – but the person who can best answer that question will be Connie herself. And it will be interesting to know what she says in five or six years' time.'

We ended our second film with a sequence that I almost didn't dare film, and could barely watch while we did. Connie, and Doreen, were now so confident that Connie asked, and Doreen agreed, that she be allowed to visit her grandfather, alone. It meant crossing, alone, the dual carriageway outside her home, the road on which she nearly died in the accident that altered her life for ever. But as she limped, determinedly, and vulnerably, across the road, we all knew it was part of a journey she had to make, and make on her own. The return from that half-remembered darkness of coma – towards a future in the light.

She's fifteen now and since the films I've seen her quite often. The BBC in Scotland is not too far from her home – and growing up has not changed her love of canteen food, particularly chips, nor our desire to stay in touch with this brave young girl and her even braver mother. Six months after the two films' broadcast we were invited, as a production team, to attend the ceremony for the Scottish Television and Radio awards – a prestigious event which I had been to once before, when 'The Boy David' was selected as documentary of the year. We asked Connie and her mother to come as our guests. We didn't know if we would win, or even get an honourable mention, but just to be listed was a great honour and we wanted to share it with our 'star'.

It was a difficult time for us on *The Visit* team, behind the scenes. The Head of Television for BBC Scotland had announced to me and top bosses in the BBC, that he thought the time had come to 'kill' *The Visit* to make way for other programmes and other teams. 'You kill programmes when they're good, before they go off,' he said.

Fortunately, the Controller of BBC1 at the time thought *The Visit* was exactly the sort of series he wanted to see on BBC screens. We believed we would certainly be given the resources to make another series. But after that, who could tell? – a gloomy prospect, in which, once again, the most depressing and bothersome factor, in the overworked lives of our tiny team, was not the difficulties of making these stress-filled stories on film, but the problems of dealing with our bosses.

We won the award – it really is a most marvellous, and slightly frightening feeling. I ran up to accept it and, tugging at my bow tie, heard myself saying something like: 'Making films like this is a rare privilege and we know how lucky we are to be allowed to film such stories as Connie's over a long period of time. I only hope the BBC will continue to recognise this and support the kind of programmes that have so obviously won your endorsement this evening.' I was about to go on when I nearly froze as I met the stern-faced look of the Controller of BBC Scotland, Pat Chalmers, sitting at a table in the middle of the room. He clearly didn't think it an appropriate time to make a public plea for the life of my little series. Too late to go back – I went on with what I really most wanted to say. 'This award is not really for us – I want to accept it, on behalf of Alex McCall, Penny Hallowes, Jan Riddell, Aileen Wild and Aileen Campbell, the team – but we are all accepting it for the real heroes of the evening, Connie and her mother Doreen.'

The lights and the huge outside-broadcast cameras swivelled to the table I pointed at to reveal the calm and smiling face of Doreen and the lovely, lively face of Connie, her hair already growing back to length, but still a long way from the waist-deep tresses she had before the accident.

Later that night, at a post awards BBC drinks party, the smoke from the Controller's cigar set off the sprinkler system and the hotel fire alarms – I found myself leading Esther, in her nightie and coat, down ten flights of stairs to the car park, in the rain, while the firemen checked that all was safe. Honours were, I think, even.

After a spell at her old school, for the past three years Connie has been going to the Ashgraig school for the handicapped – not a setback but rather a way to bring her learning and skills up to date. She still has trouble with her foot and hand. Her speech is sometimes slower, even a little slurred. Her memory is still likely to be faulty. But these are small problems, shrinking all the time now. At first she didn't want to go to a special school, seemed aware of the stigma. But now she has shown a real aptitude for dealing with the handicapped. She is particularly good with younger children, taking them to the lavatory, helping them with their tasks, chatting to them, drawing them out. She has a boy friend too. And her mother thinks they look very nice together. And she didn't notice, until Connie pointed it out, that he is handicapped. He has callipers on his legs, a weak arm, his eyesight is bad and so is his hearing. He can't go out by himself because of this. But he and Connie go to the cinema together – she becomes his eyes and ears. The relationship is charming and inspiring – and a very good example of the kind of person that Connie is turning into.

For Doreen it has been more difficult. Connie still needs her, still clings. Doreen told me: 'Sometimes I feel she is walking in my shadow, I turn and she is there. I've heard that it is quite common in cases like this but it can be overpowering. I can't go to the bathroom without her wanting to be with me. She can become quite hysterical about it and it means that I can never – or very seldom – get away for a night out. When I tried once it was all a disaster and she made such a fuss that I couldn't enjoy the night out when I finally managed to get through the door.'

Did the filming change Doreen's life? – 'Yes, but in the best way,' she told us. I must say I was deeply relieved to hear it. I had, until that time, no idea how she might answer. 'I enjoyed meeting all of you and the camera teams. They were never intrusive, I hardly ever noticed the cameraman when I was doing something with Connie – in intensive care in hospital I didn't even know they were there. I wasn't tense, although I had thought I would be. And after the films were shown I kept meeting marvellous people who were really kind and nice about us all. I had hundreds and hundreds of wonderful letters from people, many of them from families who said they had been able to face their own problems with so much more confidence after seeing our story on the screen. People would recognise us and talk about it in the bus, when we were out shopping or in the street. At Christmas we still receive hundreds of cards and little notes wishing us the best. It makes it feel as though we aren't alone, it's a good feeling. I had one man who came all the way from Newcastle to see us, he had been head-injured himself and it was driving him mad with frustration, trying to explain to his family why his whole personality had changed – his wife had divorced him because of it.

'After you had all gone home, it seemed rather too quiet at first, but I enjoyed being able to think about things on my own. In the past my life has revolved around my job and earning a living, but all this – and the questions you asked me which made me think of the answers I myself needed – has made me focus on the children, all of them, and our lives together. That's so much more important than the way it was before. Now, I'm giving time to the family, and myself. I've learned to swim and drive, I'm still pushing Connie in her learning. In fact what the filming has made me do is learn from the whole experience. It could have overwhelmed me, all of us, it does do that to so many head-injury victims and their families. But we've improved as a family because of it.

'And now we all watch documentaries and spend a lot of time telling each other we think we know how they were made. It has certainly made us think about just what goes into the making of what we used to take for granted.'

For us on *The Visit* team the most important thing has been Graham Teasdale's perceptive remark. 'Perhaps you ought to ask Connie in five or six years' time.' Connie and her mother came to the small party we threw for our friends in Glasgow before we all moved south to become part of the new geography of television, an Independent team. And we all know that we will ask Connie and, if she'll let us, I believe that her story and future progress will be as absorbing as the films we've already made about her. She's a young woman now, a remarkable one – but then she was a very remarkable child.

CHAPTER THREE

JEMIMA – CROSSROADS OF LOVE

She's nineteen now, secure from harm, cared for with love – and never able to know what in the world it is that she cannot understand, what in the world it is that, somehow, God left out of her life. She was born different, without that element that most of us are able to take for granted, she was, and is, mentally handicapped. So she became a test of love. For her devoted parents, both an agony and a reward.

When I first went to meet her she was only eleven and I felt that I already knew her, knew her story, shared her parents' anguish. But that was because the whole idea for the series had come about because I had read the story of a girl like her, a family like hers, had learned the importance, made of pain and delight, of the visits in all their lives. The girl I had in mind died, released in one way and yet removed in another, her mother, who had written so evocatively about her, left with memories and the inevitable regrets of those who mourn, and miss and almost always feel guilt. So Jemima was to be in her stead, for the first viewers of the first *Visit* programme, the girl who would give all of us an understanding of that dreadful crossroads of love that occurs in families who have to face the decision to put a child into residential care.

And we went to meet her. And she spat in my face – hard. Jemima had no speech, still doesn't. But she could communicate, by spitting, by slapping and by waving, 'flapping', her hands, an expressive, and sometimes painful body language. Even as a child, hers were the frustrated gestures of a personality, locked behind a disability, struggling to be understood, seemingly petulant in manner: but then how many of us, incarcerated by handicap, would even consider behaving as 'model prisoners'?

Her father Lynne Brooke was a good-looking solicitor living with his extremely attractive young wife, Lesley, in what would seem to millions to have been the ideal urban style; an apartment in the Barbican, views over the City of London, a pretty and bright seven year old daughter, Hannah, and a brand new, gurgling baby girl, Matilda. But once a week the whole family packed for a complicated day's outing, loaded themselves into the car and set off to visit the rest of their family – Jemima.

When we met her she had been living for two years in the fine Regency house which had once been the home of an admiral and was now converted into a Mencap residential home for mentally handicapped children – twenty-three of them. They were cared for, there, with skill and love and understanding. The staff may not have been able to cure the children – but they could care. For an outsider, the behaviour of the children would seem bizarre. They would lie down where and when they wanted – on the gravel drive, in the hall, in a corner. They would ignore the world or show intense and sometimes violent curiosity about visitors. But while the outside world may not judge the children to be normal, for them this was perfectly routine and normal behaviour. If it was a surprise, even a shock, for visitors like us, imagine the reaction of parents considering placing a child of their own in such institutional care. For the Brooke family the problem was worse. They didn't discover Jemima was handicapped until she was eighteen months old and then they determined to cope as a family.

Lesley told me: 'We had read articles about parents succeeding well beyond the predicted odds in dealing with and bringing on a handicapped child. We had friends with a handicapped baby son, we felt that we could not only cope but that we could bring out all there was to discover, really make a difference for Jemima, way beyond what all the specialists were telling us was her ceiling of achievement. We worked, exhaustingly, for years before we realised that Jemima wasn't going to be one of those *Reader's Digest* 'breakthrough' stories of success – it was another bitter blow. Then we looked for 'cures', we went to another doctor, we thought about Lourdes, even faith healing, we went through what I now know every parent in the same kind of situation does go through, knocking on every door, going down every tunnel.'

I asked: 'Were you looking for a miracle?'

'Yes, I sort of bartered with God.'

'What was the barter? What were *you* going to give *God*?'

'Oh, I was going to believe in him again, if he made her better.... I just couldn't really believe that somehow God could let it happen. I knew that lots of people had a cross to bear in life but I thought why didn't it happen to me, personally? Why didn't *I* suddenly become inflicted with an illness? Why did I have to watch somebody else lead what I felt then would be a sorrowful life, or half life? It felt like a half life, watching her, which is why I felt I would much rather it happened to me than to someone I loved, someone I actually brought into this world. I mean, I created this person, so I felt very responsible.'

There can hardly be a parent who does not recognise the cry of guilt, the pain at being selected for a burden made of both despair and love. Lesley was able to articulate, for so many who were watching, not only the understandable reaction of someone in this situation but the desperate emotional 'bargains' one reaches for. And it became worse for the loving and tortured Brooke family. Their second child, Hannah continued to grow, delightfully, but alongside the pressure of having – so often – to take second place to the needs and demands of her handicapped elder sister. It became obvious that the price of caring lovingly for Jemima was going to be paid by the whole family. By the time Hannah was nearly six – and Jemima nearly nine – the exhaustion, both emotional and physical, was complete. But every time Lynne mentioned the idea of going to see a suitable home for Jemima, Lesley burst into tears, even though she later admitted that some small, secret part of her was fantasising about what life, during the day, would be like without Jemima – but that, at the time, was buried deep, not able to be confessed let alone discussed. They went to the home in Horndean, Cadlington and Lesley still didn't admit to herself the possibility. 'I thought, it'll be all right. I'll just go on their waiting list, it's a nice place but there's bound to be an enormous waiting list, it won't happen for years. Then the social worker came round, not long after we'd visited the home, and said she'd rung Cadlington and they had a place for Jemima, and they particularly wanted a girl of that age.

'I felt cold and sick, hardly able to stop the trembling – and yet, at the same time, there was this tiny little thought whizzing around in my head, which said: "Just imagine, we're going to be a normal family, we'll be able to go out and visit restaurants, eat in public, we'll be able to have holidays away." But immediately I then felt sick, went chalk white, not able to face the thought that we were going to part with her. And then, very quickly things started happening, the doors were opening. They wanted her at the school as soon as we could get her there, the City [of London] would pay her boarding charges, her school would help, there were no holds barred and it was all galloping along – it was like ... well, like dying, dying a very slow, painful death. Everything, from that moment on seemed close to death, it was all for the last time; the last time I would wash her clothes, the last time I would do this, see that.'

I asked: 'Were you able to tell her, somehow let Jemima know that she was going away, being sent away, from you?'

There were tears at the time and tears came back with the memory I had triggered with my question. It is no part of my job, never has been, to exploit or display other people's pain. As we always do, I instantly asked if we should stop the camera – and, as anybody would, I leaned forward and offered my handkerchief. Lesley snuffled (and, of course, had a good nose blow!) and said: 'No, if you don't mind me, I think it's important to go on, and important that people understand it all.' (And that, unsolicited, sums up what has been the reaction, we've found, so many times from the people we meet on *The Visit*.) She went on:

'The night before, we packed all her favourite toys and belongings and what I hadn't realised was that she was still going to belong to me, still be mine. It was very like dealing with bereavement. I still hadn't told her, I'd said in a rather bright and breezy voice, "We're all going to Cadlington," and of course she didn't understand at all. And then a good friend said he thought he'd drive us down there and rather gratefully we just slumped with relief – I didn't dare look at Jemima during the whole of the drive down, I sat in the front and didn't look in the back. I couldn't. Nine years – and we brought them to an end, just like that. When you take a child to a nursery school and leave her for a day, you can explain that you'll be back but I couldn't explain to Jemima. Nine years, you do everything for her and suddenly I'm just going to take her somewhere, put her down – and leave.'

But love for somebody like Jemima can be mixed with the emotions that spring from exhaustion, despair, frustration – and the terrible, inescapable feeling that you have been selected, unfairly, to carry this burden. Love can be mixed with hate. Lesley told me:

'Oh yes, it can happen. I think it is very probably more common than most of us would like to admit, perhaps it is inevitable, even necessary. I didn't hate her at first. She didn't sleep, could hardly feed, but I just looked at this sad and distressed little thing – who desperately needed me. And I desperately wanted to help. But as she became bigger and the hair-pulling, spitting and slapping became worse, I used to find myself in a rage, just bent over her, yelling. It is the sort of rage that springs from exhaustion and despair and most parents go through it with a normal child but when the child is handicapped you feel so much worse, so much more guilt about behaving that way towards someone who is so basically innocent. I was always surprised when people tried to take the guilt away from me. In one way I didn't want them to. I was quite happy to carry that – I suppose as a form of punishment.'

'Punishment?' I challenged.

'Yes, punishment. I basically felt that I ought to be punished for having created her – I think I still feel that.'

'Did you ever fantasise about a future without Jemima, a future in which both the exhaustion and the guilt wouldn't be there?'

'Yes, I knew it was crazy but sometimes I would lie in bed and fantasise that she'd had one of those peaceful cot deaths, very gentle. And I'd go in and find her smiling but dead, but happy and no more crying and no more sorrow. And then I'd fantasise about the funeral and I'd wind up sobbing in the pillow and then I'd be pleased that I was going to see her the next morning.' Such was the honesty, the fullness of Lesley's answers that I found myself almost breathless, frightened a little by the clear intelligent understanding that she had of herself and her own emotions. I felt it a privilege to be told, knew that the viewers would feel the same – and I wondered if Lesley, when she saw and heard herself on the screen, would regret sharing such a private and personal area. I asked her. No, she told me, she felt better for telling me and wanted other people to understand. In real life she couldn't, like The Ancient Mariner, buttonhole every stranger and pour out her sorry tale. But she felt likely to be misunderstood, not fully explained, unless people *did* know. Like an announcement in a newspaper, like an autobiography, this would be a way to share her thoughts and perhaps feel lighter for having done so. I know she felt it helped people understand why they put Jemima in a home, took away what wasn't actually there, but she felt always was, the unspoken criticism of her action.

Lynne felt differently. He had watched his wife nearly destroyed by the experience. 'As Jemima got older I just saw Lesley diminishing with all the effort and love and attention and total devotion that she was putting into Jemima, and that hurt.'

'Did you feel guilt as well about putting her in a home?'

'I think it's a total cop-out. I feel so appalling about having my child put away. I mean it almost feels as though we're two criminals engaged in a dreadful conspiracy, that we've committed some sort of crime between us. She should be here and we should be coping.'

'But clearly that is more than you can carry, and she's cared for and loved at Cadlington.'

'Yes, I know, but we've copped out of what we thought we could do, we thought we could keep her in the family and we can't make it. And although I know it's not really a cop-out I can't get away from that feeling of guilt. And Lesley's got that guilt too and we can't talk about it to each other because if we do it very soon degenerates, and we get tetchy and start shouting at each other. It's as though we've both committed a murder and the last thing that two people who have committed a murder can ever do is to talk to each other about it.'

This conspiracy of shared guilt is not new to people like Mrs Mary Brough, the Matron at Cadlington. She's seen it before. Before a child can be admitted to Cadlington, Mrs Brough must decide if the case is suitable. She looks at the family as a whole, viewed the Brooke family that way. 'I could see that there was a lot of stress in the marriage and I felt that here was a case where we could help by having Jemima into Cadlington and it would relieve the stress at home with the parents. There's a new baby in the family, it was all proving rather too much.'

'But do you relieve that stress and then, in a way, replace it with another, the guilt stress that comes from having left their child in an institution?'

'Yes, that often happens and it has in this case. Mum particularly is feeling guilty but as time goes on they'll see that Jemima is loved and cared for. They'll actually see more than that, they'll come to understand that parents who put their children into a home like this are being very wise. After all, the children grow up and become even more of a problem as handicapped adults; and then the parents get older, less able to cope, and eventually die. If the child has been settled into a community before all that happens, it means less disturbance and emotional strain for the child.'

On the day of a visit the tension mounts. The whole family make the long journey every weekend, but Lesley still worries. 'I worry about her being cold, or hungry, or not having a coat on. When I'm with her I'm not a fussing sorting of mother, but when I'm away I do become neurotic about silly things. I have a whole different set of rules for Jemima. Why? – well, it's a different love. It's a non-developing love, a very special love. Someone, who is also the parent of a handicapped child, once said to me that it's like a very sad love affair.'

'And yet,' I said, 'she is happy in the home, we've seen her, filmed her. She is loved, and cuddled, and kissed.'

'Oh, I love to hear it.'

'But why don't you know it?'

'I suppose I always felt that Jemima wasn't going to be an easy person to love and I just couldn't bring myself to believe that anybody would really be genuinely fond of her. But I really must believe it. There's a boy in the home, one of the leaders, who has a soft spot for Jemima and she absolutely dotes on him, and once when I was there and I picked her up he was walking by and she put her arm out for him – and he took her rather awkwardly, because I was the mother and I'd only just arrived. But I smiled and he took her in his arms and she wrapped her arms round his neck and I know that I must remember scenes like that, not my own invented miseries.'

On the day of a visit, they always take Jemima for a swim in the pool of the local Holiday Inn. In the water, which she loves, all her involuntary movements become fun, and look normal. There's tea out somewhere, and Hannah, almost old before her time in these matters, helps feed Jemima, or back at the home, she helps feed other children. We filmed their day, recording the giving and receiving of saved-up love, observing the physical strain, understanding the heavier emotional strain. They played in a meadow, in front of the home, a field to charm Prince Charles, rich with wild grasses, buttercups and cornflowers – wild marguerites, nodding in great white drifts of an artist's delight. Jemima was, quite literally, a picture to illustrate an eighteenth-century poem. And then, almost in a hurry, they were packing up the car and driving back. Lesley had told me, in London, that leaving the home felt like putting the lid on a coffin. But surely not after such a rewarding and comforting day?

'No, it's not so bad now because I know we shall be coming down here again and on recent visits I've been allowed to tuck her up in bed, and every few weeks we can have her home to stay the weekend.'

Her face changed, softened into the sadness, the resigned

and beautiful expression that you see so often on the faces of parents like her, on the calm but wearied faces of nuns who work with the children of famine, on the faces of experienced nursing sisters – particularly in children's wards. 'You see,' she explained. 'My logic tells me it's all right, but while we sit in this car talking we are going further away, from her – my little girl, left behind; loved but only visited.'

The car murmured on through the Hampshire countryside. Stuart Wyld our cameraman quietly slipped another magazine of film onto the back of the camera, as riveted as I was by Lesley's articulate words. The whole reason *The Visit* series was invented in the first place was being both illustrated and demonstrated, beautifully and, clearly.

Lynne spoke: 'I enjoy the whole day, always. The people at Cadlington are wonderful, the children are beautiful and the whole atmosphere is about caring and loving and I just think we're very fortunate to be part of this scene. Otherwise it would be a whole area of experience which would be denied to us. It's almost as though I'm saying that we're glad that we've got Jemima the way she is – although I'd give anything for her to be normal – there is another side to it, which has benefited us as people.'

An admirable statement, expressing love and selflessness, but Lesley's response to it was one that would be understood and sympathised with by every viewer – and us in the car with her. She said:

'Well, I think I'd still miss the chance of meeting all those beautiful people if I could. I don't find the experience of Jemima worth the beauty of all the lovely people that are around her. I know that the handicapped world is absolutely amazing, but I'd love to have been introduced to it without having Jemima. I wish I could have found some other way. I still feel bitterly resentful that it's happened to us, and that it happens to anybody, when I see any of these children. I feel sometimes very, very sad and sometimes the beauty of the day and the beauty of the world seems to emphasise the sadness, too.

'So, when we have a good, sweet happy day it has a sort of

sorrowful side to it as well. The other side of the coin.'

There was nothing more to say, little more to learn. That's where we ended our film and brought on the end-title music. At that time it was a poignant piece called 'Jasmin', composed by Chris Hazell and played by my favourite harmonica player, Tommy Reilly, accompanied by James Moody on the piano and Skaila Kanga on harp. It was long, long, after the transmission of that first *Visit* film that I heard, from Chris Hazell, that he had written the tune (which we had taken from a long-playing record) in celebration and love for his own little daughter, Jasmin – a handicapped child.

Jemima is nineteen now. Hannah is fifteen and baby Matilda is eight – and there is an addition, Louis, a blond knockout of two years old. Lesley and Lynne both look much the same, still live in the Barbican, still commute to Cadlington and Jemima. Nowadays they have a seafront cottage (called Three Bears) on Hayling Island, just twenty minutes away from Jemima. At first, just after they'd bought it, Lesley dug her heels in because it would mean spending every weekend, and more to the point the entire weekend, with Jemima, placing a heavy burden on the whole family. But now she loves the cottage as much as her husband. The bizarre disappointment is that Jemima doesn't really love the cottage – when they fetch her from Cadlington she just puts herself to bed. At heart, it's clear, Jemima is a town girl. She enjoys lorries and cars, lots of people in the streets to flap at; flowers and grass do little for her at all. The cottage is tiny and Jemima doesn't stay overnight – except once when she fell asleep and couldn't be wakened – but she is taken back 'home' to Cadlington, at night. Lesley calls it 'shared care' and it creates problems for the rest of the family.

'Already Hannah is ducking out of some of the weekend visits – they are all devoted to Jemima and I can't tell you how proud I am of them but they mustn't become saturated with the stress of caring for her, because then they would start to carry the parents' guilt,' said Lesley.

How often does Jemima come home, to the Barbican?

'At the time you were filming we were trying to work out some sort of pattern and we gradually discovered that the longer visits were much better, so Jemima now comes home for the big holidays, Christmas, Easter, summer and so on. Mind you, Jemima doesn't like physical effort much, and Lynne is much, much better at coping with her. He gets annoyed because she walks for him and knows that she can get away with not walking for me. So I take her everywhere in her buggy, feeding the ducks, walking through the market, round the Barbican centre. I suppose the biggest difference is that I have slowly removed myself from the things I can't do with her because Lynne is better able to cope with her strength and has more authority over her. I still meet people who say 'Our child is in a home and loves it.' But we haven't reached that stage because we can't say she loves it, she may, but we don't know – she doesn't run off joyously when we take her back.'

Jemima still slaps and pinches – only now they are the slaps and pinches of an adult. Lesley was upset at the time we talked because she had recently found herself slapping Jemima back in order to demonstrate to her what it might feel like. Every so often Jemima has a kind of fit and, while that is difficult enough to deal with, the two or three days beforehand, when she is 'pre-fitting', are almost worse. The tension and strain of coping with this have become a considerable burden on their family life. Lynne works late nearly every evening during the week; 'That means that time at the weekend with him is like a gem, precious and to be protected, but it can be ruined if Jemima is having a really bad day.

'And yet you feel more awful if she's had a bad day and you're taking her back to Cadlington in the evening. That feeling of betrayal hasn't stopped, even after ten years.'

Lesley has started work again, returned to teaching, a half day every morning at the local school with infants and juniors, five to eleven-year-olds. 'So many things in our life are different because of Jemima. Because the other children grow up and one's love for them changes as they do, then that's why I went on having babies – I have the urge to care. Lynne has submerged himself in his work as a solicitor and I have taken a job. We wouldn't have been able to do that if Jemima hadn't been in the home. We've had difficult times, still do. We've even had counselling to help our marriage and I know Lynne has difficulty coping with my neurosis – I'm still having therapy for that.'

But this was not a report from a disaster area – the Brooke family are alive and well and doing better than many others, coping with strains and disturbances in their lives that might well have shattered them as a family. Lesley feels that taking part in *The Visit* film was the first and most useful therapy. 'It was as if I had hung up my pain, to watch it on television – and it lessened the sharpness of my feelings.

'I had many letters, and responded to every one, I had not had dealings with the public before and I was touched by how loving people are. Then I put the whole thing away from me but when I eventually looked at the programme again, because I hadn't seen it for so long, the first thing I noticed was how physically close I was with Jemima. I realise I went through my distancing to lessen the emotional intensity I was feeling and in letting Lynne deal with her strength we had gone through a role reversal. That was painful to realise. I had forgotten how close I was to her. But being interviewed, even as closely and intimately as I was, was actually the best thing. What I wanted to do was talk all the time. Once I'd found the benefit of release, then I could hardly stop. Even when it wasn't an interview situation, when you weren't there, I still wanted to talk. When you were taking travelling shots of me in the car, I wanted to keep turning to the camera and tell people things, like "I've a sick feeling in my stomach while we journey to Cadlington" and other things – I was actually missing the opportunity to say how I felt, and I wanted every opportunity to do that. Looking back on it, I realise it was therapy – I was using the film to help myself.

'It crystallised a great deal for me, I was able to hear what Lynne felt – not because I asked him, he might have responded with an allowance for my feelings and our relationship, but because he was talking equally frankly to you. I didn't mind about other people knowing our most intimate secrets, I still don't! I'm the sort who will confide in people at bus stops – I don't inflict my worries and fears on my friends but I was more than happy to tell a stranger.

'Mind you,' she told Jan Riddell, when I wasn't there, I hope to spare my blushes, 'Desmond does have a genuine, caring feeling about this sort of thing – he makes you feel certain that life is for sharing.' I hope she's right and I am truly useful....

We always show the films to those who have been their 'stars', the word 'participant', most commonly used in television, hardly applies with our kind of documentaries: 'partner' is more like it. I asked the Brookes to come to my home, one evening before it was due to transmit, so that they could see it (on cassette) in comfort and privacy. After we had run it, we all left the room so that Lynne and Lesley could consider for themselves, without pressure, what they might feel when it broadcast.

Lesley said: 'Once you'd all left the room we both sobbed and sobbed and sobbed. We saw ourselves more clearly than we ever had before and it broke us up for a while, it was so important that we had that first viewing in the privacy of your four walls. But then it was perfectly all right. We knew that we wanted it to go out exactly as you'd filmed it, we knew that we wanted other people to know about it all.

'After the film went out we had many letters from other parents of handicapped children, expressing sympathy, saying that they felt better able to carry on having heard that there were others who felt as they did. A solicitor wrote and said he cared deeply that I shouldn't blame myself. I remember Lynne saying he didn't want to get any letters because I think he was frightened he would get abusive letters – but we didn't get one such letter. I even had people asking me to come and stay in their homes, offering us a holiday. I was amazed at all the wonderful press write-ups and good reviews, my sister has kept a cuttings book about it all. I was a bit surprised that one reviewer called me 'this Habitat mother' – and I did get one dirty phone call because I said I was breast-feeding Matilda.'

Lesley did raise one point, a small one, important enough

for us on *The Visit* team to take the lesson firmly on board. She complained that sometimes the filming of small domestic scenes that were required to illustrate their life, took on an artificial quality – not when they were real, but when they were re-enacted. She reminded us that we had wanted to show the family having breakfast before they set out for their visit to Cadlington, but, because it took so long to organise the small convoy that we had become, by adding a film crew and production team to the party, they finally had to cook and serve bacon and eggs at lunch time. It's a good point: sometimes it is necessary to ask people to go through a simple action again, because it may not have worked technically, or they may have done it too self-consciously the first time. But I can see that if you are already in a tensed-up condition, doing something like that may seem unimportant to us, but could seem ridiculously over-theatrical to the ordinary person. We have learned our lesson.

But the most important lesson was the first one we proved on *The Visit* – other people's experiences, told simply and caringly, are the kind of stories which, on television, can teach us all.

CHAPTER FOUR

LOVE ON DEATH ROW – THE SAN QUENTIN BRIDE

She was sitting in her council house in Battersea watching a documentary about men waiting to die on death row, San Quentin. She fell in love with a multiple killer, drawn, she says, by his soft voice and gentle eyes. She wrote to him, the correspondence became a daily exchange. She decided to marry him and determined to visit the most notorious prison in the world, with her three children by her first marriage, to become the bride of a man who had been sentenced for a robbery and shooting in which he left two men dead and two crippled for life. She knew that her relatives and friends would regard her as insane. She came to us to find out if we would chronicle her visit, examine her reasons, and prove to doubters – and allow her to prove to herself – that she wasn't completely round the bend. At first sight, a story to make any newspaper editor or television producer leap into action.

But we had doubts about making a documentary about Virginia Harris and her obsessive love for the killer, Hasan Brown. She was smart, level headed, feline attractive, not mad at all. But her ambition was quite literally sensational – and did that mean that we could be in danger of being seduced into sensationalism? *The Visit* has never set out to be other than popular, never pretended to any better ambition than that of good story-telling. But we knew that the area from which we drew our true life stories was one from which all of us could benefit – in the best sense. Charities have sprung into being behind the making and broadcasting of a number of our documentaries. The viewers, seldom fewer than 6 or 7 million at a time, have – we (rather pompously, perhaps) like to think – been better informed, left wiser, hopefully warmer by their new understanding. But if we followed this story what justification could we reach for? Yes, it was a good tale. But, it was also an amazing, even a saucy tale. Not very likely to bring about good works in the wake of its transmission, or inspire viewers to behave similarly – God forbid. I mentioned my doubts to a very dear friend. She laughed. 'I've seen you in love, you were single-minded, determined, not to be deterred,' she hit at me. 'You've watched obsessive love take over other people's lives, change them completely – sometimes not for the better. But sometimes turning them into amazing people. It isn't always love for a person, it can be an idea or an ideal. But when it's obsessive it can teach all of us a lesson – sometimes it may be a salutary lesson. But who said your *Visit* programmes always have to be about hero or heroine figures?

'What drives this woman? – there isn't a viewer out there who isn't going to wonder if they might not be capable of the same apparently irrational actions, the same lunatic ambition. They'll all argue that they would stay in control of their emotions, if they were faced with similar circumstances – and in their hearts most of them will know that they, too, could succumb to this kind of madness. It is after all the madness which is celebrated by poets, the stuff of Shakespeare.'

I don't (still) agree with all that she said. It could be, in part an intellectual rationale, little different in its ultimate aim, from the murky justifications of the inky-hearted, cheque-book journalists in the tabloid jungle. But, my friend was right: I have observed what obsession in the name of love (but usually, in fact, it is jealousy or thwarted possession) can do to an individual. This *Visit* could be illuminating as well as exciting – and anyway, I told myself, we were most unlikely to negotiate permission to film inside one of the toughest prisons in the world. Nearly half of San Quentin's 3000 prisoners are in for murder, 1466 killers, and almost every week there was an outbreak of violence. (In fact, the week before we had these conversations, two men had been killed by fellow prisoners – although we didn't know it at the time.) So, we decided. And I was wrong. Not wrong to do the story but wrong to believe Jan Riddell couldn't talk the hard-nosed men in charge of San Quentin into allowing us freedom to film.

Virginia had previously been married to a jazz musician, she was born on one of the small Trinidad islands and came to Britain as a child. Now she had three delightful young sons of her own, Michael, sixteen, Jason, eleven, and Mark aged nine. She was working then as a social worker, hard put to support the family on her own – let alone find the funds for her new passion.

She had found us by ringing the producers of the documentary in which she first saw Hasan, on death row, Yorkshire Television. A member of the production team there gave her the address to write to but said they weren't interested in her idea of going to San Quentin. Partly, I am sure, because of the exorbitant costs of filming overseas with ITV union agreement – they travelled with large crews, on high wages and allowances, always in comfortable and expensive style. The BBC, on the other hand, using public money, have always sent everybody 'poor' class – we sometimes felt grateful not to be travelling on the wings. (Thank heavens Alex McCall has good friends in certain airlines where they work hard to see if they can grant occasional favours to jet-lagged working passengers like ourselves.)

Virginia had little or no money to finance her wild dream, only the thought – not uncommon in these days of chequebook journalism – that if she agreed to 'tell her story' to a newspaper or television company, there might be enough reward in it to finance the whole project. In the BBC, where it's licence payers' money we're dealing with, that's not possible and, in any event, I have always believed that documentary material which is purchased then begins to owe more to the size of the sum paid than to the element of truth that we are looking for. The whole nature of The Visit is the antithesis of 'paying for quotes'.

Virginia agreed to use some savings, and borrow a little, to pay for at least one air ticket to San Francisco (the nearest city to San Quentin) but she also had three children who had to travel with her. British Caledonian came to the rescue, with much reduced rates for the children. It was a great gesture and my gratitude was marred by Virginia then asking who was going to pay for the wedding dress – and the ring! She pointed out that Hasan, already twelve years served into his sentence for murder, wouldn't have any money and she produced what, over the future weeks I was to see quite frequently, a little-girl, winning smile. I felt, what over the future weeks I was also to feel quite frequently, irritation – and wondered if my first instincts about staying away from a rather sensational story had been right. But I think I was being unreasonable. We, as a matter of honourable responsibility, pay our *Visit* interviewees a low standard sum, agreed by the BBC as being enough to compensate and reward them for their effort but not so much as to influence the content or their response. We also pay out-of-pocket expenses when people lose money by staying away from work in order to film with us, or when we are using their home or supplies in the course of our filming. So, I reflected, it may be the first time that 'Wedding ring and wedding dress, for ceremony in San Quentin' had featured in BBC accounts. Somehow, I knew at the back of my mind that Virginia wouldn't forget to remind me of the hotel and meal costs – and, to my credit, I had already decided that *The Visit* ought to buy her a bridal bouquet for when she walked up the aisle, or is it along the prison gallery, or is it through the cell corridor? How did I get into this? I began to think.

But Virginia truly was a remarkable person, with a remarkable obsession and she had survived for years, without a husband, bringing up her children on her own – and bringing them up admirably. And she had been lonely. She told me: 'My daily life is empty, completely empty. My children give me a lot of joy but when they go off to school or when they've gone to bed in the evenings, then I feel the need to talk – and there's no-one there to talk to. I want to laugh and there's no-one to laugh with. Yes, it's lonely.'

So, for the twelve months before we met her, there had been a daily letter, sometimes more than one a day, received from Cell 3W70, San Quentin. And each day she wrote a letter back, sometimes two, always many pages long. The outpourings between two people, the one incarcerated for crime, the other locked in domestic loneliness, grew into millions of words.

They even spoke on the phone. Prisoners in San Quentin are permitted to use the pay phone in the main cell block – Virginia paid for the calls, her bill became astronomical and she was once, while we knew her, cut off! She took it in good humour and remarked that, quite frequently, the price of true love must be a disconnected telephone. At home in Battersea, it seemed hard to imagine the fierce conditions at the other end of this transatlantic *Romeo and Juliet* tale. San Quentin makes no secret of its reputation – the men sent there are among the worst of America's criminals, consigned to die, or confined for life.

Hasan Brown, one of seven children, two brothers and four sisters, was thirty when he received his first letter from Virginia. He had been sentenced to death at the age of nineteen and after eight years on death row, only because of a change in State law, his sentence had been commuted to 'life'. Only two years after that they started executing them again in San Quentin. There had been a pause of several years during which many states debated whether to keep the final sanction at all and in most of these it's now back in place. Hasan knew how lucky he'd been and how close he'd come to death in the gas chamber, at the hands of his fellow men, by order of the law. Since then, during his time as a prisoner, he'd survived a number of prison fights, and stabbings, in which two other men had died. He'd become a survivor.

It isn't easy to get into San Quentin, as a visitor. In the week before we filmed three men were killed in riots and fights. Jan Riddell flew to San Francisco and started the mammoth task of battering her way through the barricades of American bureaucracy. They lock men like Hasan up for a reason and even family visiting rights are strictly controlled – filming permission is very rare and the kind of access we needed to follow this bizarre romance was almost unprecedented in their experience. But I think even the men in charge, who must have seen and heard most tales by now, and certainly seemed inured to any romantic appeal, were intrigued by the bizarre nature of this love-behind-bars story. If Hasan wanted to put in an application to marry then, under prison regulations, he was

48

entitled to a visit from his bride-to-be, entitled to wed her if all the papers and documents were in order – and we could be present, as also could members of the family. If Virginia wanted, she could go ahead with her personal folly – and, if we wanted, we could follow the story. Over the transatlantic phone I asked Jan: 'But what is Hasan like? Are we locked into some kind of madness, here?'

'No, come and see for yourself, he's the opposite of anything you might imagine when you think of a man who has killed two people while committing a crime.'

On her say-so, we booked the crew and flew to California. Virginia and her sons were due to travel out later. I went to visit Hasan. And I met a small, neat, gentle person with large soft eyes and a low, careful voice. Not a villain, not an obvious murderer. (But then, I told myself, do any of us really know what such a person would look like? Is there a stereotype, outside the pages of Hollywood's central casting agency?) He told me:

'In August, 1983, I was filmed by a documentary team who were doing interviews with men on death row – waiting to die. I knew they'd taken that film back to London to broadcast it, I never knew when it did go out, only that (out of the blue) I started to get these letters from Virginia. And I looked on that as being a gift from God. Here I am in the penitentiary, right here in my own home town, and I can't find a female. The other men they can have visits from girl friends and, if they're married, their wives can come up and spend time with them, in the evenings and at weekends, in a group of special caravans they keep here for that kind of visit. So it was a gift, do you see.'

I asked: 'But when you received the first letter, before you had talked of marriage in a letter, before she had got that far, at the time of that very first, out-of-the-blue letter, didn't you sit in your prison cell and think to yourself that this was some kind of nut writing to you, drawn to you, as she said because of what she felt you were, through the television screen?' A long question, too long for use in a film, revealing more about my doubts than his.

49

'No,' he replied. 'I saw it as more of a pen pal thing. And one thing led to another.' Short answer. Who anyway would ever dare try to analyse what it is that makes one person fall for another, how it is that love grows 'from one thing into another'? It was time I stopped making a film about my own perplexities and buckled down to the simple task of telling somebody else's story. Hasan had tried to shoot his way out of the ghetto. Now, there was no way out of San Quentin, except by serving his time – a lifetime. And why should he question anything that entered his life from the outside, any relief from the inescapable routine of prison – certainly the only kind of escape he was likely to achieve for many years to come? In the pressure cooker that is San Quentin, Virginia's letters became his contact with another world. And which world was the more real was not the point, after a while prison existence begins to feel like the fantasy and the letters the reality. He went on:

'About the fourth or fifth letter she began to tell me about her love relationships with other men and I started telling her about mine. I fell in love with her mind at first and then we started exchanging pictures and it became a physical attraction.'

And so it grew and she said 'Yes' and he said 'When?' and they spoke on the phone at great length – and cost – and she thought about getting to 'know' him better in the family visits, ten days every few months, in a caravan, among other caravans, in a prison yard, surrounded by thirty-foot walls and barbed wire and electric wire and armed guards. . . . Hardly a honeymoon concept, rather a conjugal concession, arranged because it also suits the prison not to have any more pressure to deal with than they must. And she thought about the time that Hasan may be released on parole, many years away, and would she live in America, the wife of an ex con, and a murderer. And would he be a stepfather to her children, and would that give her pause for thought?

And still she was determined. We interviewed Hasan's mother, Edith, living in low quality housing in Oakland, a giant, sprawling and cheerless satellite of San Francisco. She's

50

a strict but loving mother, and grandmother. Her husband left her in Ohio when Hasan was two years old and she came west looking for work to support her large family. Now she lives on welfare and tries to bring her children up in the same churchgoing manner she has always maintained. She knows she hasn't succeeded, particularly with Hasan, christened Lance and known to his whole family as Peeky.

'He was always bad, mischievous bad, but bad. He was really an enjoyable little fellow, crazy, kept everybody laughing but he got his share of whippings. I had switches in every room because I believe in switches. Belts don't work, shoes don't work, your hand doesn't work – switches work. And you know people say to me these days, "the way you whipped Peeky, why is he where he is now?" and I don't know, I really don't know, because I taught my kids "Thou shalt not steal" and you don't cuss – and you don't kill. But on the streets here it's a jungle. It really is. It's kill or be killed. And that lesson is the bad one and the one he learned – and he's paying for it now. He's done wrong and he's in the penitentiary, serving his time. My Peeky, that's what he'll always be for me – even where he is.'

Virginia was convinced that Hasan would be eligible for parole within a year or two – he'd served twelve years and that, for her, seemed long enough. But she was deluding herself as Steve Perez, one of the correctional officers, as they're called, at San Quentin told me: 'To be honest with you I think Hasan is looking at another ten years inside – he'll be likely to serve a total of not less than twenty years.

'Remember that at his trial there were a total of five charges of murder against him and some of those were in the first degree. And he was only released from death row because of a change in the State law. He would have been executed, without doubt, otherwise. And people are not going to forget his crime, and community leaders are involved with the parole board and they aren't about to let him back in the community with his record for violence and death.' Some American prisons are motivated by ambitions for rehabilitation, San Quentin is about punishment. By the time a man has reached those grim, steel-barred galleries – housing the most violent of America's criminals like condemned battery hens – there is no thought of recovering him as a useful member of society. Society wants rid of him, locked away, dealt with and forgotten.

Another senior prison officer at San Quentin, Fred Everly, also knows that some women find excitement in having a relationship with a man in these circumstances: 'It's a bit like the romantic concept of being involved with an outlaw or a highwayman. It's a sense of romance connected with something that's not available to them in ordinary life, being married, or lover to, someone who has to live on a razor's edge. Sometimes the inmate discards the woman when he gets out. She's been useful in bringing him packages, being there in the caravan for his needs, but once he's out he usually heads for the bright lights and the fast life – and dumps the poor thing who paid the monthly sum of money to him while he was serving his time.' A bleak and caustic view of life, from a man hardened by many years of experience.

'Perhaps Hasan is different? Virginia certainly thinks so.'

The cool eyes swivelled towards me and rested, unblinking, on mine. 'If he is different, then it's the first time I've known it be so – you get all types in here, but not too many miracles.' I knew it was no part of my task to let Virginia know the doubts that years of experience would bring to bear on her hopes – to shatter them. In any event, she was locked into her romantic fantasy, obsessively blind to any criticism or reported failing in the script she saw ahead of her, the story of a 'prisoner's moll' in which she had happily cast herself in the leading role.

Virginia flew to California, tumbling off the plane, wide-eyed and tousled, accompanied by the children – all of them, nevertheless, sparkling with excitement. They checked into a small hotel, jet-lagged, disorientated and, perhaps therefore, more than prepared for the unreal experiences ahead of them. The next day she travelled to San Quentin – our patient and forbearing production assistant, Aileen, 'baby sitting' the three children – while she waited, with the other 'relatives' for visiting time, at the gatehouse to San Quentin. The metal detector shrieked and she was parted from her belt (with buckle), her wired bra and her shoes (metal buckles) and hand-searched, then allowed to dress again. Not a foolish precaution when you think of the 3000 desperate men in the prison, all serving long sentences, all for crimes connected with violence, most of them the kind who wouldn't think twice about using a smuggled weapon, or knife, to fight their way out of the place.

Although it was to be their first meeting, Hasan had already applied for permission to marry, filled in all the forms, been through the clearances. Virginia had been security cleared by the FBI and the British authorities. She could change her mind if she felt differently after the first meeting with this man she had so far only known as a signature on a letter, a voice on the phone – and a small tattered snapshot. Hasan had created a kind of shrine in his cell. On the top bunk – men with records like Hasan's are always given cells to themselves – he had arranged a row of photographs, piles of letters and cards, all in all an icon, created to adulate a person who had so far only lived through her own description of herself, had never been measured in his world, in reality.

They ran across the huge family meeting room to each other, ignoring other prisoners, armed guards, our film crew. No reserve, no holding back, no shyness. For minutes they clung to each other, a crow bar couldn't have prised them apart. Then they sat, in a corner, holding hands, whispering – for the three hours until visiting time was over. Over the next week they met four times and then it was the first Tuesday in the month. And that is the day, each month, when inmates of San Quentin may be married. A lady member of the prison staff who is also a Justice of the Peace is called in to perform the brief – but legal – ceremonies. Hasan wore smartly pressed jeans, with a knife-sharp crease in them, a sign both of an old hand and an inmate who works in the laundry. Virginia wore a wedding suit, her children their best clothes, and she carried two wedding rings, one for each of them. The future was going to be that way: whatever they needed she would have to provide it for both of them. Virginia had a small wedding bouquet and looked, particularly for the mother of three sons, shy and demure.

And so, in a small glassed booth, rather like an enlarged phone box, we all crammed in – and Virginia was married to Hasan. The boys looked solemn, more a reflection of the new surroundings than a reaction to the occasion. Mark, aware somehow of the strangeness of it all, frightened by the threat to his future, cried. Virginia hugged him, whispered comfort but soon turned back to Hasan. After the ceremony we left them, taking the boys with us, while they sat and held hands again in the dusty, institutional, visitors' room.

Three days later, the couple were granted a five-day honeymoon in one of the caravans, parked in the prison yard, almost directly underneath the windows of the room that houses the gas chamber. A week later Virginia was back in London, Hasan sitting in Cell 3W70, each writing screeds to the other. Husband to wife, wife to husband. She knew that it might be years before she saw him again; she knew it might be many, many years before he could even be considered for release. Her obsession remained, unswerving in its romantic aim.

'I know I'll have to wait, in the meantime I'll have to save so that I can make another visit next year. It's been worth it – everything I thought has come true, there's been no disappointment, no let-down. I know that everybody, my relatives most of all, will think I have been mad. I still don't see it that way. I've had my dream – and it's come true. Now, for lots of people that never happens. So you may think I'm mad to start planning on possibly living a life in the States, waiting for him to come out, being near to him so that I can visit regularly and we qualify for "time out" in the caravans.'

Oddly, one part of her folly of love could have been possible. Obtaining a 'Green card', which enables one to work for a living in the States, is one of the hardest tasks for an immigrant – no problem for the wife of an American citizen. Hasan, convicted murderer, serving life in San Quentin, was still an American – so, therefore, was his wife. But Virginia, dreaming of impossible futures, of small bungalows, comfortable jobs and the dedicated image of a woman 'waiting for her man' hadn't taken the children into account, her relatives, his relatives, and the total absence of any funds in her life. It was a dream. She was determined. Such things have happened, she'd already proved that. It seemed unlikely, but none of us on the team were prepared to bet against it happening.

We stayed in touch after our return to Britain. Virginia, being Virginia, still had expenses well beyond her income – and still had her 'little-girl' request, could we help? We did what we could, within the tight restraints of a BBC budget and my personal reluctance to avoid being used as a 'soft touch'. She asked if her 'story' mightn't be worth something to a newspaper, at about the time we were due to broadcast it. I was reluctant to see her go down that route, knowing that the kind of tabloid that would be interested in paying for her personal story wasn't likely to be squeamish about the manner of its printing, the prurience of its detail – or the blackness of its headlines. In the end, most reluctantly, we passed on to her – we had no right to withhold it anyway – an enquiry from *The Star*. They paid for her story – she didn't seem to mind the sensational layout and the concentration on her sex life in the caravan. She assured me that it was worth every penny, being saved towards her next trip to San Quentin. It was still not completely possible to resist her, or her dream. . . .

Five years later ... Hasan is still in San Quentin, still not eligible for parole, still serving his life for taking a life. And Virginia is still in Battersea, working as a registered child-minder now, her boys grown considerably, two of them working, only one left at school, but all of them still living at home.

And Virginia and Hasan are no longer married. The dream is over, the romantic obsession has been shattered. The marriage lasted just over a year, Virginia still saving to return, both of them still writing. But Hasan wanted her there more often, she had made one return visit a year later, taking with her one of the children. After that Hasan became demanding (shades of advice from the San Quentin prison officer), and Virginia became torn between her responsibilities to her children and the tugging of an impossibly romantic notion. Then the letters started to change in tone – and finally Hasan revealed that the marriage was not legal. He had been married before and both he and the prison authorities had thought the papers connected with his divorce were in order – but they weren't. No marriage. Her solicitor confirmed it. It also turned out that Hasan's previous marriage had been while he was in San Quentin, to the sister of a fellow convict, all of which went to underline the thought that, for the authorities at the prison, such romances were little more than a method of taming and quieting some of the more notorious inmates. This sequel we've pieced together from California and London, Virginia is naturally not happy about discussing, in detail, an episode that for her has ended badly.

But she still has no regrets, none at all. 'I would do it all again. After the programme people stopped me and said – Good on you, you show 'em.– Yes, I'd do it again tomorrow, I'm not ashamed of any part of it.'

Had it killed the romantic side of her? – 'Not at all, I still think he was a lovely man, I hope things work out for him. God hasn't dealt him a good hand. As for me, well, I'm alone again, there is still something missing in my life. And perhaps it is that I have to find a friend, or a lover, or a husband. All I know is that I definitely don't want to be on my own for ever and a day – that would be one of the worst things that could happen to me.

'Hasan's family have stayed in touch with me and that's really nice. During the hurricane in this country, his mother rang to see if I was all right – and when there was the earthquake in San Francisco I phoned her to make sure they'd all come through it.

'I didn't find the filming an intrusion – and the answer to anybody who thinks it wouldn't have happened without the camera being there, doesn't know me. I'd have done it, somehow, no way not. I even had letters from people who were contemplating the same thing, marrying someone in prison, and my story had helped them sort themselves out. I

Connie and Doreen today

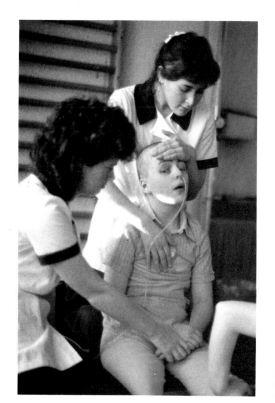

TOP LEFT: *Connie, in hospital, out of coma – but still in physiotherapy*
TOP RIGHT: *Connie with Shakin' Stevens mementos*
BOTTOM: *Connie home from hospital, with Doreen, her mother*

TOP LEFT: *Jemima with her mother*
TOP RIGHT: *Jemima today*
BOTTOM: *Jemima when we first met her*

TOP: *Hasan behind bars in San Quentin*
BOTTOM: *First meeting of Hasan and Virginia*
OPPOSITE: *Virginia*

Mass start of the swim

The mountain cycle section

The marathon section, with wife and son urging Don on

End of the Triathlon

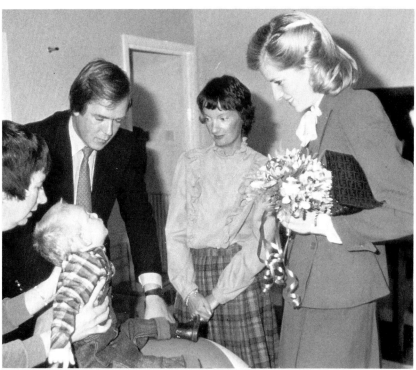

TOP: *Jamie and the whole family*
BOTTOM: *Jamie and parents with the Princess of Wales*

sent all the newspaper cuttings to Hasan and now I kind of regret that I don't have them to remind me of what I did. I wouldn't mind reading them again.' She paused.

'But the letters, his letters are a different thing. I haven't been able to read them again. One day, I must sit down with a strong drink and a cigarette and go through them again. But, I do confess, I haven't the heart at the moment. It will be like tearing myself apart.'

Weeks later, Virginia contacted us again. She has now been written to by Hasan's new lady (one he may have known before her). Not a friendly letter, but patronising and hurtful. She distrusts Hasan now, thinks him a liar and a con man, doesn't want to hear his name again. Her hurt is obvious.

She told Jan that a poem by Spike Milligan reflects her feelings nowadays. I think that, in choosing it, she still reveals the romantic pitfalls in her own nature.

THE NEW ROSE

The new rose trembles with early beauty.
The babe sees the beckoning carmine.
The tiny hand clutches the cruel stem.
The babe screams.
The rose is silent.
Life is already telling lies.

CHAPTER FIVE

TRIATHLON MAN

He'd nearly died under the surgeon's knife – and now he was prepared to kill himself, as a way of saying 'thank you'. He had contacted us, wanting the publicity for his cause, prepared to put up with – perhaps enjoy? – the exposure of his personal life, his very personal battle, but still a battle which he could lose, and lose publicly.

Don Clark, probation officer, hardly seemed the stuff that giants are made of, but giant**killers**, like David with his Goliath and Jack with his beanstalk, have always existed in both our mythology and history. And they continue – the little league football team threatening the big boys, the cussed individual taking on the developers, the school child beating the chess champion. Don told me: 'I know it's madness, but I have been operated on for a spinal tumour – the odds were heavily against me even surviving, and even then it was odds on that I'd recover paralysed from the chest down, in a wheelchair for the rest of my life. So, I was so pleased to find I was alive and able to walk – albeit with one leg not properly functioning because of damage to the motor nerve – that I decided I wanted to say thank you to everybody in the neurological unit at the Atkinson Morley's Hospital, in Wimbledon. And I wanted it to be something more than a box of chocolates for the nurses, signed "A grateful patient". Which is why I've come up with this madness – I've already run the New York marathon for charity but now I'm going to take part in a triathlon, raising money for equipment for the Atkinson Morley's.'

A triathlon is a killer, by anybody's terms, they don't give them names like 'The Iron Man Triathlon' for nothing. It is, as the name suggests, a three-pronged event of immense and fearsome challenges – a 2-mile speed swim in the sea, a 75-

mile bicycle race through mountains, a marathon of 22 miles, all one after the other, all without pause, an almost inconceivable test of stamina and strength and survival. Don's idea would be to spend some months training and acquiring sponsors who would guarantee money for the hospital on the basis that he completed the course. He was not deluding himself into thinking that he might come in the first bunch: indeed, he pointed out one of the rules that said of the final leg, the marathon: 'Competitors must only compete by running, jogging, walking – or crawling. Any other method means disqualification.' Crawling, Don joked, was a distinct possibility when talking about a 22-mile run, after a 75-mile cycle race, following a 2-mile swim. Perhaps I was wrong to be so impressed. But, after all, I suspect most people are more like me than like Don. Swimming ten lengths of the local pool would half kill me, wobbling 3 miles on a bicycle on the flat would certainly finish me off – and running for a bus is more than I like to do.

We met to talk about it. Don is a smiling North Countryman, with long blond white hair – irritated at times by people telling him that he's a Jimmy Savile look-alike. But he admits the comparison is accurate. He was working as a probation officer in Brentford, a job he enjoyed and was clearly good at. He was married to Marjorie, a bubbly, red-haired Scottish girl, twelve years his junior, a flight purser with British Airways. He was forty-three, pushing it as an age to run a marathon, pushing it to the limit as an age to attempt the triathlon. But worse, this was a man who admitted his doctors had told him not to overdo things, who liked a pint of beer, or several, and smoked thirty cigarettes a day. Marjorie had taken up running in order to accompany him on his training sessions – 'I'd never see him if I didn't do it with him' – but still, from time to time, ran alongside him yelling, 'You fool, it's suicide.' But, she admitted, without any real hope of persuading this single-minded (to the point of complete stubbornness) man to give it all up.

They met when he was a civil engineer, pulling down houses to make way for new roads. He began to hate what he was doing, troubled morally by some of the insensitive decisions he was forced to administer. He decided instead to go to university at the age of thirty. Marjorie helped keep them both while he qualified for a social science degree – she used to give him fifty pence every day, to attend Kingston Polytechnic in Surrey. Probation officer is a tough kind of social work, not always applauded by the public or appreciated by the 'clients'. Don had a delightful eleven-year-old son, Sam, from his first marriage, who spent holidays and weekends with his father and Marjorie.

Three years after they married Don developed severe back-aches. He eventually wound up being told by senior consultant neuro-surgeon, David Uttley, that he had a spinal tumour – and only a fifty-fifty chance of coming through an operation, and then with an even greater chance of being paralysed for life. He went through with it – 'I didn't have much of an option, did I?' – and after seven hours in the operating theatre, he was cured. It left damage to his left leg, and he was to develop hip trouble (he is now anticipating two hip replacements). His walking was erratic ('I have this tendency to fall down'), his running even more so, but he came out of the whole drama alive and not paralysed, his faith in himself intact. Marjorie's faith in God had been restored. Before the operation, she sat miserably at his bedside in hospital. 'Yes, I prayed,' she told me. 'I don't believe there are any atheists in fox-holes, are there? When things look at their worst you latch on to something to believe in.' Afterwards Don developed his obsession – a useful and entirely supportive obsession – with raising money for much needed micro-surgery equipment, of the sort that had saved his own life. He raised £10 000 in the New York marathon, the committee of the Friends of Atkinson Morley's told him he was mad, but backed him all the same. They probably thought he had been a fitness freak before the operation – the opposite was nearer the truth. Don remembers starting his running training:

'I had seen this documentary about the famous Jim Peters, at the Commonwealth Games, staggering into the stadium in Vancouver and collapsing just before the finishing line, and I so admired his superhuman effort that I thought if he can do it then I must try. So I started training. My first run was horrific. I ran out of my house and down the street and I started to think I was dying within the first few yards. There's a mark on a garden wall to show how far I got that first day.'

'How far was that?'

'Would you believe about three hundred yards! After that I used to go out in ordinary clothes so that if I had to stagger to a stop I could pretend I was just walking somewhere, or looking in shop windows or something like that. But there were still times, in those early days, that were unbelievably embarrassing. Once I was overtaken *twice* by an old lady with a shopping basket and she said to me with great wisdom the second time, when she passed me heaving on the wall: "You'll bloody kill yourself, you will." The first time I managed to run a mile without stopping I felt like Roger Bannister – and it took me about 10 minutes.'

As his training progressed, so did his enthusiasm for running. He took an interest in a sports shop, The Running Bug, selling high-tech running shoes and T-shirts. He sold me the most expensive pair of trainers I've ever bought ... He started a club, called The Stragglers, and they used to meet in a Kingston pub, where Don shocked all the fellow members by continuing to smoke. He even had one burning in his fingers when he told the others that he was going to enter the triathlon, in Nice, France. My own evangelical passions as an ex-smoker probably made me harp, while we were filming, on why he didn't give it up. I was much encouraged by Marjorie to do so. Finally I asked him, on camera, if he thought his much adored son wouldn't have a better example of a hero figure for a father, if he didn't smoke. Don told me: 'If I saw Sam smoking that would make me give it up at once, but I do believe that he won't be tempted. He has a slight asthmatic problem anyway, and I think he understands that I think it's wrong but still do it. He thinks it's disgraceful that I do smoke.'

By now we were filming regularly as this paradox of an amateur athlete picked up the pace of his training, started recruiting sponsors to reward his attempt to finish – or kill himself. We were also negotiating with the organisers of the triathlon, a really heavy business. Such events are completely sewn up in advance by sponsors and municipal representatives and the television 'rights' have long been sold to a company, such as Smirnoff. It was all big league for us, too big. There was no way that a small documentary team, with a limited, and strictly controlled budget could compete on the basis of 'buying in'. Just covering the event would, in any case, be an 'all hands on deck' situation for us. We'd clearly need a second film crew and director in order to follow our man through all three parts of the race.

We approached the organisers with our problem and an offer. We wouldn't get in their way, we'd always take second place to the main film units, who would be concentrating on the front runners. Our hero was clearly going to be a very long way behind the top international names who regularly dominate the first five or six places, names that are spoken with awe and respect in triathlon and marathon circles. But – and we bent no knee to commercialism or sheer buying power, on this – our man was motivated in the most amazing way to earn charity money for the most worthwhile of causes. This meant that in the race was somebody running for truly good and selfless reasons – and that might not be a bad image for the triathlon to have. We had heard stories from The Iron Man Triathlon, held each year in Hawaii, about the mighty American ABC network, employing 'minders' to stand near each of their film units – and throw out any other film unit. There had been smashed equipment, battered technicians belonging to small teams who had just thought that it would be all right to film the event for their local station. At this stage, our loyal and immensely hard-working production sec-retary, in Glasgow, Aileen Campbell, revealed that she had taken A-level French at school. She had been listening to me trying desperately to think of 'how to deal with bully boys' phrases in French. Thus she produced a list, largely unprintable in this book, to embrace my desire to cover such situations as: 'This rubber dinghy has been promised to me for an hour, kindly leave it be'. And 'It is my turn to take a shot from the organisation helicopter – kindly put that cameraman down, and stick your head up a dead bear's bum'. And 'If you hit me again, my friends in the NKVD will visit your home and see to my revenge.' And one or two simple ones, like the Anglo Saxon; '— off' and '— yours'. It enlivened an evening and left me rather thoughtful the next morning. We had clearly entered a television league beyond our normal experience. My friends in the BBC Sports department laughed and told me even more horror stories about fights to protect purchased television access when newcomers entered the scene. But Jan Riddell won a number of significant assurances from the organisers and their sponsor, the Coq Sportif sports goods manufacturers.

We planned to enlist the help of the talented John Pettman, who had been working with me on *The Marriage* series and had also done a couple of *Visit* films as director. (He and I first met when he worked as the number one film director on *That's Life*, earning himself a reputation for splendid film-making – and never being off the telephone. We also planned to take both Aileens from Glasgow and so, with all of us working, we would be six in total from production, and another seven making up two film crews and an extra cameraman. Most television teams were fielding outfits as big as 200 or more. We comforted ourselves – size isn't everything – and worried.

Meanwhile Don had put up his training limits, running ten or more miles a day, pushing himself to 60-mile cycle rides on his special Peugeot professional's bike and swimming at least 1 mile a day. He left his home in Teddington and the training in Richmond Park and went to Loch Lomond to test himself on mountains with his bike and in cold water with his swimming. Both nearly ended in disaster. Alec Hunter, leading light in the British Triathlon Association, went there to coach him. On a mountain road, swooping downhill, Don braked, skidded and fell off just in front of an oncoming car. Uphill pedalling may be harder work, downhill at speeds of up to 60 miles an hour is much more dangerous. He learned to apply the brakes and release and apply and release, rather like a car's self-operated anti-brake-locking system. In the water, he nearly froze. There was little he could do about it except hope that, on the day, in Nice, the Mediterranean would be warmer.

We all flew to Nice several days before Don, Marjorie and young Sam, desperate to see his father do well, were due to fly in. We were booked in to a very small, back-street hotel – BBC allowances wouldn't even run to the price of a meal in one of the big hotels on the Promenade des Anglais. But we went and had a drink in the Negresco, with the organisers. Three gin-and-tonics and two Coca-Cola's cost me £20. I began to worry some more. By now we had become desperately fond of both Don and Marjorie. The more we saw of the amazing, near-professional competitors from the international triathlon circuit the more obvious it became that our hero was walking out into a Roman arena – to face the lions. But our little family arrived, Marjorie confessing to me: 'What do you do when you love someone to pieces and you know they're going to go out there and risk themselves? – I'm not sure I'll be able to look. But I don't want him to know it. I admire him for all this more than I can ever say.'

They drove round the mountain course with more than thoughtful expressions – it gave me the jitters just looking over some of the unguarded precipices from the little open-top Citroën we'd hired to use as a film car. We'd also arranged for our second cameraman, Denis Borrow, to film, sitting side-saddle, from the pillion seat of a motor cycle – a truly hair-raising prospect. The sea was cold, too cold. And to cap it all Don was having trouble with his hip and had arranged to have a cortisone injection straight into the hip-bone just before the race, which would kill the pain but probably not for long enough.

On the morning of the race we were up at dawn. The weather report was fair but the sea temperature was colder than ever. At the doctor's, we filmed Don receiving his injection – and joking with us about his hip-replacement operations. (He has every intention of continuing to pound along with his running, even with replacement hips and, when told that he could wear them out, like motor parts, he told the surgeon that he'd come in every so often for 're-treads'.)

TRIATHLON MAN

On the beach, an hour later, he slathered himself with grease to guard against the cold water, they stencilled a number on his arm, gave him a swimming cap, easily identifiable in the water, pointed out the life-savers in their rubber boats and on their surf-boards – and 392 men and women, from twelve countries (forty-five of them from Britain) ran into the water and set off. The top athletes expect to be back on shore for the cycle section in about 45 minutes: we hoped that Don could do it in less than 2 hours. Around the seafront start John Pettman and a full second unit filmed the background shots and Alex and I filmed from the ground. Within an hour there was trouble: scores of swimmers were being pulled from the water, suffering from hypothermia; dozens more had been stung by shoals of giant jellyfish. The top athletes were back in 41 minutes, changed and pedalling away only minutes after that. But in the changing rooms underneath the Promenade des Anglais, scores of doctors and nurses worked desperately to revive the swimmers – Don among them, dragged from the water semi-conscious and half frozen. Ninety-two swimmers needed medical treatment. Don had completed enough of the swimming section to be allowed to continue – we pleaded with him not to: the film was unimportant, his life was. His answer was to borrow a cigarette from one of the medical attendants – and light up. 'It's important to me, I've got to do it,' he told me. 'But thanks all the same, Desmond.'

He limped out shivering to the bike park and climbed into his skin-tight cycling shorts. Twenty minutes later we were crowded into our little open-top car, with me at the wheel and a considerable amount of unneeded advice, such as 'watch out', and 'for God's sake' from my other passengers, as we hurtled after the cyclist section round the hairpin mountain bends.

He completed the cycle section comparatively quickly, even yelling at us that it was all a 'piece of piss', as he sped through one village. That sudden expletive, not deeply shocking, but greatly surprising coming from Don, broke us all up. He had, cheerfully, hurled at us the encouragement Alex McCall had been hurling at him, all the time we had been filming in

Scotland and Richmond and on that daunting reconnaissance through the mountains behind Nice. Don may have been stretching himself even beyond his limit – but he hadn't lost his sharp sense of humour. We had Marjorie and Sam with us, jumping out at every bend, as we leap-frogged past him and waited ahead for our film shots, they were there waving him on. Never has a competitor had such support, such waves of love urging him on. Then, with eleven miles of the cycle section still to go, we heard that the whole race had been won, in 6 hours 5 minutes and 22 seconds, by Mark Allen the American champion. Another American, Dave Scott, was second, only 36 seconds behind the winner. And Don still had about half an hour's pedalling ahead of him before he could start the 22-mile run. It was no more than we had expected but it served to underline the huge difference between the capacity of these highly trained professional competitors and this brave but inexperienced hopeful.

He started the final section in fine shape, lolloping along the promenade, protected from the holiday traffic by straw bales, followed by us, rooting for him to make it, fearing for him as he tried.

By the 11-mile mark – half way – Don was staggering, the organisers were closing down the route, taking away the vital straw bales, shutting the refreshment stations, where the athletes could pick up a drink or a wet sponge. They had told us that, as an exception to the normal rule, they would leave the finishing rostrum in position. By now, more than a hundred of the competitors had dropped out through injury or collapse. As Don sat, panting, at the half-way mark for a 2-minute rest – we had to send our motor bike off to fetch an ambulance for another competitor, who fell almost at our feet. When Don set out for the return 11 miles, they must have seemed like a hundred.

Five miles from the end, dusk falling, Don staggering and slowing, Marjorie jumped from the car and ran alongside him. It's allowed in the rules, although having a full-time pace-maker isn't. Two miles from the end, one small boy couldn't stand it any longer and he jumped out and ran alongside his Dad, as well.

Half dead, swaying and stumbling, the lines of strain and exhaustion etched on his face, Don crossed the finish line, 3 minutes before the race finally closed officially. He had finished in nearly 12 hours, 6 hours behind the official winner – but a winner in everybody else's book, including ours.

And at the prize-giving the next day, much to his surprise, the organisers made particular mention of his effort and awarded him a special prize. The next day we flew home and Don started collecting the money from his sponsors – he didn't get £100 000 but he did make nearly £10 000, we were all disappointed for him. But he described it as 'a painful learning curve' and clearly felt that it had been very well worth while. We felt more, he had set himself a personal challenge as well as a charity target – and he had succeeded in that, brilliantly.

We heard from Don quite often after that. He and Marjorie came to see the film before it transmitted, and enjoyed it. Don had quite clearly caught the 'sponsored event' bug. He talked of cycling through Africa, were we interested in covering it? I thought of my bosses in Scotland and their faces if I suggested such a mega-budget as we would need, and I decided I had taken enough risks on this one already. After the film went out, more money rolled in for the hospital, all of which served to endorse Don's efforts for them.

By then we were working on other *Visit* films but we did hear, with considerable surprise, that Don and Marjorie had split up. She has since married again and has had a baby, he has met and lives with a fellow worker in the probation service – but they've both given up probation work. In fact, they both rode a tandem across America, collecting money for charity and live now near Leeds.

I suppose it only proves how little you really do know people, when we discovered that Marjorie was having doubts about their marriage, even at the time we were filming and at a time when she was being particularly loving and supportive to Don in his risky and strenuous folly. Don didn't know then, either. 'It came as a bit of a shock later,' he said. 'The difficulty was that the film went out some nine months after you'd shot it and by then Marjorie and I had parted, I had met Mary at an office party, her marriage was in a bad state and had just broken up – and we got together on the rebound. But it's all worked out for the best and I couldn't be happier. But, back to the time you transmitted the film, the week it went out a lot of people recognised me in the street and called things out, and then I'd see them do a double-take on Mary, who clearly wasn't Marjorie. So, for the first weekend after the broadcast, we stayed indoors all the time. But it's all okay now.

'Looking back on the whole episode I certainly felt I learned a lot and don't regret suggesting myself. I do regret not making more money for the charity but that was no-one's fault in particular. I certainly didn't mind the viewers – strangers – seeing all my effort, even see me being pulled from the water. I felt at the time that it was all among friends and funnily enough I still felt that when it broadcast. Remember that just before the broadcast, my marriage was breaking up and subsequently broke altogether and I was thinking about my job, and where I was going to live and what I was going to do for a living. And I felt, well they can take away your house if you can't pay the mortgage, they can take away your job, if you don't do it well enough – but they can never take away the fact that you've run in the New York marathon AND you've competed in the triathlon.

'When you stopped filming it was quite peculiar at first, I missed you all. There was an emptiness and nothing to put in its place. There had been a buzz, an excitement and then nothing. But when I first got back from New York after competing in the marathon there I found myself out in the park running and I thought "Why am I doing this, there's no need to now". But, of course, there was a need. I'd started a way of life and it was worth keeping it up.'

Now Don wants to raise £1 million for head-injured children, by riding right round Britain. He may do it. Don Clark is still a man looking for challenges.

CHAPTER SIX

FIGHTING FOR JAMIE

He was dead. Nothing would bring him back. Now his life was being celebrated, in music, in verse, with prayer, with song and with fond recollection. A thanksgiving for Jamie. Very proper, very comforting for those left to grieve, clinging to their memories, finding solace in the measurement of good times past. But he was only seven, had barely started on life's path. And for all of his own short span he'd spent it in a world of darkness and silence, an angelic-looking boy – a deaf blind boy.

On a fierce winter's day, the morning after a storm had (for the second time in a few years) felled thousands of trees, ruined houses, killed people, I drove past wreckage, round fallen timber, through floods to the warmth and comforting atmosphere of Beaulieu Abbey, in the New Forest. Alex and I stood in the lovely church, thinking of the child whose life had changed our own, whose story had touched the hearts of millions. A surprisingly happy day – all the sense of loss compensated by what we knew he, and we, had gained. I smiled at his parents, across the church, they smiled back and Jane gave a little wave. It wasn't a funeral, children were singing with spirit and joy, adults were smiling (some through their tears) and the old, mellowed stone walls looked yellow and bright in the lamplight, as the last remnants of the winter storm spluttered to an end outside.

When I first met Jamie he was almost exactly the same age as my youngest son, Joshua, two and a half. They even looked very similar, both blond, with smooth clear skin, happy personalities and a huggable side to their natures. It wouldn't, in any event, have been hard to like Jamie, with his gentle hands waving, waiting for a touch, the stillness in him while he worked out who was holding a hand and 'writing' on his palm. We had been drawn in to Jamie's life through SENSE, a remarkable organisation for the Deaf Blind. (It used to be called The National Association for Deaf Blind and Rubella Handicapped.) Now its new name and its famous Royal Patron, The Princess of Wales, have done an enormous amount to increase public awareness and understanding for the deaf blind, a condition much more common than many people think. Their Chief Executive, Rodney Clark, and I had met when I first also met a remarkable young man, Graham Hicks, who, wherever he went was able to create a sense of awe in most people because of the calm way he simply and coolly overcame his devastating handicap – and went on not only to work for SENSE, but to raise funds for them, speaking through an interpreter. Rodney had told me that the biggest problem for the deaf blind was actually discovering the extent of their condition, then finding somebody who knew enough to help them. Parents spent years not properly knowing what was wrong with their child, desperate for expert diagnosis and then skilled training. SENSE had a small residential centre in Ealing, Middlesex. There parents came with their child to spend two or three days, undergoing intensive tests, then learning how to cope with the results. He took me to meet Lindy Wyman, in charge of the team there, a dedicated and determined woman, she regularly produced what most parents regarded as little short of miracles.

We agreed that if she found a child and parents looking for assessment and guidance – and they agreed to being filmed – then it would make an illuminating *Visit* film. It would, they most hoped, bring in the parents whom they knew to be 'out there', not knowing who to turn to. It would, for viewers generally, I felt, literally illuminate a world of darkness and speak for a world of silence. And so we met the Rogers – and Jamie. And the film we made warmed us all and touched our hearts more than usually. We called it 'Fighting for Jamie'. And now, five years later, brave, loving, Jamie had given up fighting – exhausted, perhaps, by the strain of living so painfully, step by step; happy, perhaps, to slip away from those who loved him and struggled with him. Jamie was dead, quietly in his sleep, his breathing, always so difficult, just stopped.

Jane and Peter Rogers were a successful, loving couple, living a sunshine life on the island of Lanzarote, in the Canary Islands. He was a partner in a villa owning and renting firm, managing good-quality holiday homes, with care and skill. They both loved their life on this strange island, with its dark volcanic beaches, and the friendly local people. They already had two bouncing and attractive daughters when Jamie was born, in a local hospital. Emma was five and Lucy just a year. Jane told me:

'I think with Emma I just couldn't believe that I'd produced anything so incredibly perfect, and then I had the same feeling again with Lucy, even though she was a second child and you don't expect to feel that "magic" way twice. So, I just never thought about having an imperfect child, I always expected my children to be perfect. I know it sounds slightly stupid but you always think that things like having a handicapped child happen to other people, not you.' She and Peter had been through nearly every test that doctors could devise for Jamie. They were in London to arrange a stay at the SENSE home in Ealing, they were about to go back to their island home, and they invited us to live with their experiences. Generously, they wanted to ensure that we were well looked after as well.

We flew to Lanzarote, hired uncomfortable little jeep vehicles to transport the equipment and checked in, not at a hotel, but into several of the charming villas owned and managed by Peter's company. It felt like a holiday setting, making the documentary task ahead of us seem slightly unreal. Normally, on location I tend to take a 'studio' room which leaves me short of bedroom space but also leaves an area for meetings and discussions between us all. We often visit the supermarket and all chip in to buy carafes of local wine and peanuts and 'bits'. By tradition it has become known as the Desi-bar and actually serves a vital function while we're on the road, allowing us privacy to talk among ourselves, plan the next day's shooting, share doubts, criticise each other – or just unwind – without being in the public circumstances of a hotel bar, and paying the hard-to-justify-on-BBC-expenses prices for drinks in the bar. The price we paid for this useful and pleasant accessory to our travel was always paid by me personally. I am a tidy-minded person (my family think me obsessively so) and I would gaze ruefully, at the end of an evening, when everybody had departed to their own rooms, at a room full of dirty glasses, a bed covered with peanuts and broken potato crisps, and – worst of all – overflowing ashtrays. I put up with it, but self-pity prevented me from doing so without complaining, which I did frequently. The villas gave us living rooms for the first time in all our travels. Alex and I shared a villa but on this occasion Jan and Aileen Wild decided they would like to be responsible for the crew bar. They bought exotic salamis, salads and hot dips, covered the lights with red material, lit candles and called it 'Slack Alice's'. It certainly worked for unwinding but wasn't quite the right atmosphere for production meetings.

The Rogers lived in their own house, a little way from the tourist front, dramatic views, cool rooms, an enticing swimming pool. It was the perfect setting for an achieving couple and their family. For two years it had, in fact, been the site of painful, dedicated therapy and training for Jamie – a place where the Rogers' nanny, Mandy, worked tirelessly and conscientiously with the little boy who lived in a world, almost beyond our reach: a world of darkness and silence. Jane knew, sensed almost from the moment they first showed her Jamie, in the hospital, that something was wrong with the son she knew her husband had so wanted.

'Yes,' Peter told me, 'I wanted a son – and I've got a son.'

And his love and pride shone through, without any qualification or reservation, determined by Jamie's handicap. He went on to tell me how they had first discovered the handicap and then how they had begun to uncover its frightening dimensions.

'We were worried after a few months because Jamie wasn't reacting in the right way to various things. Basically we worked out that he wasn't reacting to light and he wasn't reacting to sound – and at first we wondered if there might be a natural explanation for this (some kind of delayed learning or slowness) but by the time he was three months old we knew it was serious.'

Jane added to that: 'We were lucky in a way because although we suspected all this at three months we didn't get the final diagnosis until he was nine months old and we had time to prepare ourselves. So, it wasn't someone saying to us: "Your son's blind and deaf" and that's that. But nevertheless, the shock of confirmation is still bad, when it happens. It makes you wonder about all sorts of things.'

'Does it make you wonder if it might not have been better that this child hadn't lived, in the first place? Can a parent think these things?'

'Oh, yes,' Jane told me, with that startling and almost overwhelming honesty that she has (and which I have found in so many of the *Visit* parents, in similar cases). 'I think people who say they never think like that would be blind themselves. Every time Jamie was ill as a young baby I suppose at the back of my mind I thought, "Gosh, perhaps it would be better if he died." But then when they are ill you fight like anything to make them better, you think to yourself: "There's no question that he could possibly die, he mustn't die, he's mine and I want him to live – I love this child so much he must live." The first time I went through that, then after, somehow I knew I had accepted Jamie as he is and would go on fighting for him all the time.'

Peter pointed out: 'There is another element. Because Jamie is deaf and blind you think all the thoughts that Jane has talked about but you also wonder what quality of life is Jamie going to have? Remember that by then we had discovered that not only was he deaf and blind but he also had floppy muscles and was mentally handicapped, considerably retarded. But now look at Jamie today and how he is beginning to communicate, and see how loved – and loving – he is and you know that all the effort and work has been worth while. And you also know that Jamie does have a life and it does have a quality to it. And I don't think, looking back, that we would want to change anything.'

Jane added: 'You see we did sit down and we said to ourselves, "Right, we've got two girls and they're just about perfect, and we've got each other – and, if we want, we can sit here and cry for a week, but that won't help Jamie. The only way we can help him is by doing and getting on with just about everything we can." And after a while we found ourselves at Great Ormond Street waiting for some brain tests on Jamie and we met a number of other children with devastating problems and we discovered we were saying to ourselves: "Aren't we lucky, Jamie is only deaf and blind."'

We filmed the careful and strenuous routine that the devoted Rogers family – and Mandy – had worked out. Therapy with Jamie, testing his hearing, constantly testing and pushing to see if there was even the smallest residual capacity left, ringing bells, rattles, horns, electric hooters. The same with his sight, glistening paper, shiny objects, bright lights – searching all the while for some reaction, and getting none that they could be sure of. Jamie was difficult to feed, all his food had to be puréed and then put into his mouth, a spoonful at a time, pushed down, to make him swallow it, by inserting a dummy into his mouth – a messy, spluttering and seemingly risky business. Then, the girls were constantly being drawn into specially devised games of blind man's buff, playing tests to see what they could identify by smell or touch or taste. They had their ears covered and then had to ask questions without being able to hear. All of this was designed not only to give them a better understanding of the world their young brother inhabited, but to encourage them to help with his care and training.

By now, Jane and Peter had become – as far as reading books and talking to doctors could help – self-trained 'experts' on how to deal with the deaf and blind, and how to deal with Jamie. But they knew they weren't expert, they knew they needed to know more, to know if what they were doing was right. They came to England, and Ealing. We flew in with them.

The meeting between the Rogers family and Lindy Wyman, at Ealing, was charged with the family's understandable nervousness and eased by Lindy's wise experience. They spent the weekend assessing Jamie. A number of impressive 'specialists' used sounding devices, dark rooms with lighting effects and patterns, callipers and braces to determine his capacity to stand even if it meant being supported. The whole family joined in all these sessions, sat round for hours in question and answer sessions of their own, worked with blindfolds and ear muffs to demonstrate how well they could empathise with Jamie's world. Also, Lindy's team were able to study Jamie as he behaves at home. We had agreed to transfer, to video-tape, all the 'rushes' we had shot on the island regardless of whether we intended to use them in the final film. This gave the clinic the opportunity to study the equivalent of many more hours of Jamie's behaviour than it would normally be able to in a brief visit. It gave us the opportunity to be helpful and useful to this admirable family. There are those who may feel that, like wildlife film crews not interfering with the 'red in tooth and claw' dramas of the jungle or the pampas, we should hold ourselves back from the situations we film, otherwise we aren't reproducing a completely, clinically true picture of what might happen to our subjects. These people, for my money, must live with their criticism. None of us would ever want on our conscience the thought that we withheld any help we could offer in cases like this. We're not there to change circumstances with money, or mighty influence, and then film that change, but neither are we there to behave in a cold-spirited way. The criticism has been put to us in the past, usually by people who have never made a documentary of this kind, and we have been firm in our rejection of it. Sometimes even sharp-tongued.

At the end of that first assessment Lindy was able to tell the Rogers family: 'I've seen the video you took of him at Lanzarote and I think he is on the brink of a great deal.' I was watching Jane, saw her slowly expel her breath, as someone does when a heavy weight is lifted from her shoulders. Lindy went on: 'He's obviously listening to something, his eyes appear to be looking at something. We don't know what yet, and won't until the end of this long weekend.' She told me later: 'The other thing that is very clear to all of us is how much his parents care and how caring and loving they are, and how much they manage to do. So, from his parents' point of view I think we have to point out how much they've done and how good it is – and just try to build on that.'

'Will that little family be able to leave here, then, with the beginnings of a language, a way to communicate between themselves and Jamie?'

'But they already do have a language, they have their own communication system. And if what you mean is a structured language then the answer is, yes, we're already talking about that with them and when they leave here they will be equipped with a formal language they can teach him – and he can talk back in.'

Then began three more days of tests, checking responses, charting indifference – or was it fatigue? And how difficult it is to tell when the subject's lack of response may be inability or straightforward – refusal. But there were moments of pure magic. We were actually filming when Jamie 'tracked' with his eyes the sideways movement of a group of silver Christmas tree balls on the end of a short stick. He did it twice, positively. It meant that he did have some kind of sight, possibly only the capacity to tell light from dark, possibly more. Whatever it proved to be it was a world of difference between the total darkness of the completely blind, it gave everybody a corner from which to start, a new way of talking to Jamie. Jane was in tears, but so were the team – and so were we.

They went on to discover a very low level of hearing, but nevertheless hearing. Jamie would always be classified as deaf blind but the tiny little perception he could use in both senses would make a fundamental difference to the whole of his future life. He would be able to tell night from day, recognise bright objects, perhaps even colours. He would be aware of the world of sound, realise that the 'touch' language on the palm of his hand was substituting for that. The family started learning the phrases that they could develop into a language for Jamie: 'Bath Time.' 'Go For Food.' 'Have A Bath.' And many more.

They were nearly finished with their first visit to the centre when there was a 'Royal' day. The Princess of Wales arrived on a visit, she had been told about Jamie, knew of our film – we had been asked to brief her lady-in-waiting and the press secretary, before the visit. Jamie enjoyed the sniffer dogs who determined he wasn't made of semtex, and the Rogers waited in one of the training rooms, Jamie balanced on a large bouncing ball, Emma and Lucy, getting on with some drawings, at a school table. He looked edible when the Princess came in, I was only surprised she didn't pick him up and hug him; we had explained that this would be his only understanding that anything out of the ordinary was going on. She clearly wanted to cuddle, and chatted for a long time with Jane and Peter and the two girls. Jamie giggled through it all – and nobody ever found out if he even remotely understood what was going on.

There are estimated to be 5000 families in Britain with deaf blind children. The centre can only deal with about a hundred families a year. They know there must be many times that number 'out there' in the community, needing help like this – and not getting it.

During this visit the Rogers took Jamie to visit a leading paediatric consultant whom they had been visiting since Jamie's birth, Dr David Ogilvie. Until this trip he had never been able to tell them exactly what it was had caused Jamie to be born deaf blind. He now had the results of many tests and they showed that Jamie was suffering from Leber's Blindness Condition, not manifested unless the Leber's component is transmitted into the child from both parents. So that although both Emma and Lucy are normal there is always a four-in-one chance that any future children will show the same condition, and Jamie's progress would never be better than about a fifth of that of a normal child. At ten he would 'be' a two-year-old, at twenty he would still not have reached the development of a five-year-old. It was a shattering confirmation of many fears that up until that time Jane and Peter had been able to avoid facing. But within minutes they had recovered their normal, cheerful ebullience. They returned to the centre in Ealing, buoyed up by the diagnosis of Jamie's capacity. Lindy told me:

'There have been golden moments throughout the weekend, the moment when he "tracked" the silver balls, but also the moment when his fingers started to play with a toy cube, and he was clearly recognising what he had, and would know it again. But the truly important thing has been the atmosphere for the whole family and the fact that we've been all together, they and us, together in mind as well as physically together.'

She went on: 'And the other thing is how close we've been with all of you, on the team, and the film crew and it has felt like a special, happy, family reunion, the best atmosphere, marvellous.' A large and gentle smile of satisfaction, well deserved, hung on the face of our friend and cameraman, Alex Scott. He had, with everybody on the crew, filmed uncomplainingly and most sensitively, the whole time. I felt very proud of them – and of Lindy's praise for us all.

And there the film ended, with Jamie continuing to progress – and us staying in touch.

During the next five years we heard quite frequently from the Rogers, who had become very much our friends. They moved from Lanzarote to the New Forest in Hampshire. They made the decision because Peter was able to run his business on a 'commuting' basis and because this country was able to offer more facilities and resources for Jamie, better schooling for the girls; and it would mean they were nearer the specialists and doctors they needed to consult more frequently. Jamie progressed to a point where he was able to wear hearing aids – which he frequently pulled out and threw down – and glasses to enable his limited vision a chance, particularly with nearer objects. But he still had to be fed the old way and his chest was weak from the curvature of his spine; the likelihood of an operation to improve that was remote because of the risk to him of going under anaesthetic. But a way of life emerged, Jamie had a place in it but didn't dominate it to a point where the girls suffered. He was a brave boy, in hospital twice with pneumonia, he fought back even when doctors had warned

Jane that there was practically no hope. The girls loved him, enjoyed 'talking' to him, helping with his training, looking after him – although by now, five or so years later, he was a large seven-year-old, not so easy to pick up and handle as a baby.

Life wasn't easy for Jamie. He died because a piece of food may have lodged deep in his throat or obstructed his lungs. In the past he may have had the energy to cough the obstruction clear. But Jane now thinks he died really because he had fought long enough and was finding the whole process of living too tiring, he just decided to leave. Jane has gone back to work now, as a teacher's helper in a kindergarten class, she's taking a correspondence course to achieve the necessary qualifications to be a fully qualified teacher herself. She looks back on the making of the film with pleasure. 'At first we were a little doubtful, worried about having our private life splashed on the television screens – but after we'd met you all and talked about what the programme might achieve, what you would want to learn from us, rather than 'exploit' out of us, then we really wanted to do it. The effect after it broadcast was rather nice, it made some of the doctors seem more interested in Jamie, people talked to us in the street – it helped strengthen us with the long, weary business of training Jamie. I used to say to the girls, "We'll get Jamie up and running – and, when we do, the first person I'm going to ring up is Desmond and tell him, ask him to come and film it." But we knew that with his spine and his lungs it was most unlikely, still we kept trying, you have to.'

She added: 'But there was intelligence there, he would pick up his cup. It may sound like a tiny thing but for all of us it was enormous. He loved swimming, used to scream blue murder if he was taken out of the water. He would often just lie there smiling, waiting for a kiss and a cuddle. We never used to say "If Jamie's still here next year," we always took it for granted that he would be. I knew his lungs were weakened by having had pneumonia and the post mortem revealed that he had obstructed one of his lungs with a lump of food which he had inhaled down into it – I suppose it was always part of the risk because of the way, the only way, we could feed him by pushing food down his mouth. He wasn't with us when he died, he had gone into care for the weekend. We had evolved this system that he was looked after every other weekend so that we could devote alternate weekends to the girls, it was only fair. I nearly didn't put him in that weekend because it was Emma's birthday and he would have loved the party but then I thought that I really couldn't cope with twenty eleven-year-olds and Lucy and Jamie. But it was okay for him, I know. He must have gone to sleep, happy. He wasn't in hospital with tubes being poked down him and constant monitoring disturbing him.

'Emma and Lucy miss him desperately, but they are quite happy for him – they even pointed out that he would have a lovely Christmas. I had been quietly dreading the prospect, frankly and I was surprised. But they said to remember that it was Jesus's birthday and there would be an enormous birthday party in heaven. They also have this vision of heaven as a perfect place with a blue sky where their dog who died will now be running around with him, and their auntie Vy, who died will also be there. Emma is perhaps a little bit past that now but both girls still go down to his grave and talk to him and tell him things like: "Jesus will send you back, if you're naughty." And, you know, in many ways it was going to be a difficult time ahead for him, it's almost as if he knew that. He was getting bigger and more difficult to handle and the school he was at was about to get him into a local boarding school – and that would have left a huge gap for us to cope with. He was going to have to be pushed around in this new wheelchair with straps, which I really didn't want to put him in and he was facing the prospect of a very difficult operation to straighten his spine, he would have to be in plaster for four months.

'And it's almost as though he had said, "Blow that, I don't want any of that," and had just gone. I'm glad he had such a good life, he experienced a lot, he went riding, went to fun fairs, played on the beach – there weren't many things he hadn't experienced in his short life. I have no regrets, none at all.'

But Jane does miss him in a way that creates a real absence in her life – and Peter's. The children are nagging her to have another baby; for obvious reasons that would be too big a risk. They are seriously considering trying to adopt a Romanian child, the waiting list in Great Britain, and the age restrictions (you're too old at fifty to be an adoptive parent – it happens to be just the age I was when Joshua was born!) are against any success in this country. Jane is a determined woman – I think she will find her new baby. She said: 'After eight years of being a mother to a kind of permanent baby I feel redundant. With ordinary children they get you used to the process of separation by growing up, but with Jamie that wasn't possible. He's gone now and I've looked round and the other two don't need me (in the same way) so I must do something, care for someone.

'He was only seven but by God he had a lot of friends. After the *Visit* programme we had so many lovely letters from people, and while he was here in England he made scores of friends. He made such a difference to our lives, I really think he was the "best thing" that has happened to us all.'

In the Abbey, schoolfriends of Emma and Lucy sang special hymns, chosen by the girls and the whole family. Lucy and Emma read, so did Lindy, down from London to celebrate the small child she had first spotted as a winner. One of the poems, 'Heaven's Very Special Child', a sweetly Victorian piece, was read, beautifully, by Emma. It is now – all of it – carved on Jamie's headstone (they had to order an extra large one because of it) in the peaceful churchyard, in the quiet of the New Forest.

HEAVEN'S VERY SPECIAL CHILD

A meeting was held quite far from earth
'It's time again for another birth,'
Said the Angels to the Lord above.
'This special child will need much love.'

'His progress may seem very slow,
Accomplishment he may not show;
And he'll require extra care
From the folks he meets down there.'

'He may not run or laugh or play,
His thoughts may seem quite far away.
In many ways he won't adapt
And he'll be known as handicapped.'

'So let's be careful where he's sent,
We want his life to be content.
Please, Lord, find the parents who,
Will do a special job for you.'

'They will not realise right away
The leading role they are to play,
But with this child sent from above,
Comes stronger faith and richer love.'

'And soon they'll know the privilege given
In caring for the gift from Heaven.
Their precious charge, so meek and mild,
Is Heaven's Very Special Child.'

CHAPTER SEVEN

THE WILL TO WALK – THE RAGE OF P.C. PHILIP OLDS

He sat, in a wheelchair, in the darkened sitting room of his specially adapted bungalow, pounding the metal frame at his arm, his face twisted, glowering with rage and frustration. His eyes radiated hatred – and despair.

'I call it the pram because I don't want to call it the wheelchair. I call myself a cripple because that's what I am. I'm not disabled, I'm not temporarily out of function. I'm a cripple. I'm crippled by a gunman's bullet.'

His fury, his agony was directed at me, at the camera – really at the world, perhaps at God. It was unfair, grotesquely so. But fate often is and when it selected Philip Olds as a victim and a hero it took on more than usual, an adversary rather than a target. A victim to fight back, take on the world, driven by dark forces, hate, resentment, revenge; tortured by knife-like memories and regrets. He was a tall, good-looking, London policeman when he was shot down and paralysed by a man trying to rob an off-licence in Hayes, Middlesex. As he lay, dying he thought, on the ground, his assailant kicked him in the head and the ribs. There were two men, Hell's Angels, subsequently arrested and sent to prison. Not for murder, their victim lived. Not for a lifetime – that sentence was reserved for the man they nearly killed and, instead, paralysed. Philip Olds had been told by doctors that he was lucky to live, had much to be thankful for. He was decorated by The Queen and the police found him a new job. The beautiful girl he'd met since he was shot had told him she loved him, what had happened was in the past. The future, their future, she promised him, would be one of loving, one in which he would have much to enjoy. But he would not let it be over, he felt he still had much to fight against. His raw energy, sharpened by bitterness, was directed at an impossible ambition – to walk again.

I first read of Philip Olds in the newspapers and then read, later, of his astonishing ambition in *The Daily Mail*. We had been talking for months of the letters I had been receiving from men and women who had suffered paralysis and were now confined to a wheelchair life. But here was something different, a man who refused to accept the wheelchair as being his total existence. He was sensible enough to know that there was no cure for a severed spinal cord, nor was there likely to be one in his lifetime, but he also knew that if he could stand and walk, just a bit, each day the psychological benefit would ease his personal pain to a point where he could, perhaps, follow the advice given him by all the specialists in the field, which was to come to terms with his wheelchair. No longer a 'pram', a prison, but a fact – and a life bigger than it, and beyond it, still to live.

Philip had heard that an eccentric, scientific genius called Jerry Petrofsky, working with a group of dedicated assistants, had turned Wright State University, in Dayton, Ohio, into more than a place for learning – it had become a Mecca for the disabled. Petrofsky, a bio-medical engineer and computer wizard, was pioneering a system of electrical stimulation, programmed by a small computer, which would jerk and kick dead and paralysed muscles back into a simulated 'life'. Combined with a specially designed body and leg brace, people could leave their wheelchairs, walk, stand, climb stairs, even dance. Clumsy, slow – but for the paralysed 'guinea pigs' on his programme these steps were as vital and 'giant' as the first ones taken on the surface of the moon. His volunteers were nearly all students who had been injured in accidents. Philip had heard of one particular student, Nan Davis, who, on the day that she received her graduation diploma, left her wheelchair and walked to the podium – accompanied by rapturous applause and closely followed by the huge, hovering bulk of Jerry Petrofsky (he must have weighed well in excess of 200 pounds) carrying a handheld computer, with wires attached to his patient's legs, punching in the coded control commands for each and every, history-making step.

The London copper was determined to do the same and *The Daily Mail* had flown with him, on a trial visit, to Dayton to assess his suitability for the programme. We had been contacted by friends of Philip who suggested that it might make an ideal *Visit* film. There were just two problems – not small ones, either. The story was heavily billed all over the newspaper as a *Daily Mail* exclusive. And Philip was still a serving policeman which would require the permission and co-operation of Scotland Yard's press office. The first organisation was renowned for 'protecting' its exclusives as violently as necessary. The second was not renowned for liking the press or media it was set up to deal with. Their reputation was for refusing information rather than delivering it.

I set Jan the task of contacting Scotland Yard's press office while I telephoned my old Fleet Street colleague, Sir David English, editor of the *Mail*. David was more than willing to co-operate, provided we didn't 'scoop' his story of the moment that might come when Philip walked, by handing out our footage to the news programmes. We agreed to share some of the travel costs. *The Daily Mail* had, until that time, been totally supporting the cost of flying Philip and his fiancée Vanessa Perkins to and from America. And so we found ourselves 'in bed' with *The Daily Mail*. More to the point, we found ourselves co-operating with a talented and charming reporter, Andrew McEwen, who had accompanied Philip on the first trip and seemed set on being the constant biographer for this hero-turned-guinea-pig. By then the photographer assigned by *The Daily Mail*, almost permanently to this story, was another highly likable man, Graham Wood. Both men proved to be the best friends we could have had during the many months ahead. Andrew for his fair-minded wisdom and somewhat wry sense of humour (on this story we found a sense of humour was a must, even a rather black one); and Graham for his irrepressible energy, constant jolliness and the biggest fund of 'I remember when ...' stories I've ever encountered in Fleet Street.

Jan, our researcher, had different problems. She contacted

Scotland Yard and asked to be given the home telephone number and address of Philip. She carefully explained her purpose, talked of the previous programmes in our series and sent over a video of 'The Boy David' story, so that Philip could judge for himself if he wanted to be filmed as well as followed by a newspaper. We waited patiently for some time, then we reminded Scotland Yard of our request, by then three weeks old. 'Soon' we were promised we would have an answer. Philip was considering the matter, would be viewing our tape any day now. Some weeks after that we rang again. 'The answer is no, he's seen the video and doesn't want to do it, he doesn't mind being in a newspaper, the publicity doesn't bother him – he just doesn't want to co-operate with you lot. Sorry.' I could hardly believe what Jan told me. Already David English and Andrew McEwen had said they thought Philip would quite enjoy the whole process of filming – he liked company and this ensured that he wouldn't be as lonely as sometimes life in his wheelchair forced him to be. We asked Scotland Yard if they were quite sure they had fairly put the proposition and if they were absolutely sure that Philip had actually seen the video of 'The Boy David'. Their answer was crisp and dismissive. They were sure – and that was that.

I am cursed with a suspicious mind, a legacy of my own days as a Fleet Street reporter and the memory of a number of experiences of dealing with the Scotland Yard press office. (These days it is a very different and much more co-operative matter, since the idea that policemen can speak quite well for themselves and the thought that not all media people are double-crossing stereotypes, has become more accepted in the Metropolitan Police.) I asked Jan to see if we could get hold of Philip Olds's home telephone number and, as they always say in the spy movies, we called in a couple of favours. We rang Philip at home. She asked him why we had failed to interest him and why he thought we couldn't make a film about him as interesting as the one we made about 'The Boy David'. 'I don't know what you're talking about. I'd love to make a documentary, it might help other people, not in wheelchairs, understand. And it might give some hope to people like me, who are in wheelchairs. And I remember 'The Boy David' film, I saw it at the time – and I thought it was wonderful, I'd love to help. What's the problem?' She drew breath and explained what had happened. 'I suppose I should cover up in some way,' he told me. 'But I'm not going to. Nobody has been in touch with me – draw your own conclusions.' We did and we acted on them. I spoke to a fairly senior man, more in sorrow than anger, and suddenly we had permission from Scotland Yard. Through this incident I came to meet Assistant Commissioner, Hugh Annesley, a true diplomat of a policeman, now the Chief Constable of the R.U.C. and living in Belfast. He was to remain our loyal friend and supporter over the next two years, although at the time we had no idea how long the filming would stretch to.

The ambition that consumed Philip was not, he knew very well, a cure. The possibility of re-joining a severed spinal cord was many years away, and still is. But the sheer exercise that resulted from having dead legs jerked into life by electrical stimulation, the whole toning-up programme on exercise bicycles and other machines, that the guinea pigs had to go through, had positive benefits for the young people. Jerry Petrofsky had no intention of taking on the 'establishment' in this area, the consultants who worked for years with patients, teaching them, in Stoke Mandeville among other places, how to make the best out of life *in* a wheelchair, how to come to terms with paraplegia or, even more difficult, tetraplegia or quadraplegia. Said Jerry: 'If they're happy with that lifestyle, then fine. But if they have the will to walk again and they really want to get out of their wheelchairs then that is the common denominator we're looking for on this programme.'

What was also appreciated by the experts on the programme was that their guinea pigs would improve in general health, muscles no longer atrophied, bones returning from the fragile brittleness that develops after paralysis. Jerry Petrofsky pointed out that, for the average patient in a wheelchair, in the United States, the medical cost to the nation that stems from the lung, heart and organ diseases that develop from an inert, unexercised body, can be as high as $1.3 million, *per patient*.

Philip had met, since being shot, a beautiful girl, a sergeant in the police, Vanessa Perkins. She had fallen in love with the man who was determined to stand again, but not because of that alone. The wheelchair was the least of her considerations, the man was the first thought. She told me:

'I fell for the man, not the heroic reputation (Philip had received several previous commendations for courage, before being decorated by The Queen) nor was it the man in the wheelchair, sympathy for the disabled. No, Philip has a magnetic personality and I could see that he was fighting an enormous fight. So, I didn't take him up like a crusade, I loved him from the moment I saw him and, quite frankly, I thought "I'm going to get him". I accepted Philip for what he was from the moment I saw him. It's as simple as that.'

And so they became engaged: Philip the third generation policeman in his family, and Vanessa, also a third generation to serve in the police. And the police gave her time off to accompany him on the trip to the States – and the one to come, now he had been accepted as the only British guinea pig on the Petrofsky programme. A story of courage and fortitude – but there was a black side to this, one that disturbed me greatly. During the first interview I had with Philip in his bungalow he had talked to me of what might happen if he failed, of what darkened, and even dominated, his thoughts so much of the time.

'During my time in the force I have been injured a number of times, I'm only 5 foot 10 inches and weigh about $10\frac{1}{2}$ stone, it's inevitable. I've even thought of death, death by the bullet, through my head, my heart. If I was shot I had always anticipated that I might die – I had never anticipated that I was going to go through something worse than death.'

'Is it worse than death? Are you sure?'

'Oh, yes. Take it from me.' He was almost snarling, 'Don't take it from people who've made some sort of life for themselves, from people who've got the courage to say that life in a wheelchair makes no difference to them. And they've found themselves and they've found God, and they've found all sorts of things. I've found nothing. And I've lost everything. So don't damn well say to me that I'll get some kind of inner strength from being a toxophilite (they're keen on archery at Stoke Mandeville) or a stamp collector or wheelchair table tennis or anything else. I don't get anything from this wheelchair. I was a motor-cycle-riding, fornicating, beat-walking, criminal-catching cop – and now I'm locked in a bloody pram. Oh, yes, it's worse than death.'

'Won't you ever come to terms with it? Shouldn't you try for your own sake?'

'No, I've tried and it won't work. They didn't kill me, did they? They robbed me.'

'Robbed you of what?'

'Of death. I can't live with the frustration. At the moment there's maybe several million people who will watch this telly and read the newspaper stories and will want me to succeed – and for them I will, I really will. I'm the only Englishman on the programme and I have to do it.'

'I think your quality of stubborn bloody-mindedness will drive you to succeed.'

'What if I told you that I was frightened stupid by all this, would you understand?'

'Yes, I would. But what exactly is it that you're frightened of?'

'I don't want to die and I think I will if I fail.'

'Why?'

'Because I'm going to do it, that's why. I'm going to do it.'

We had been told that most spinal-injured patients went through a phase of deep despair, like this, that they grew out of it. But I was worried. It seemed to me that the thing that actually drove Philip *was* the despair; he used it to prime his energy. It wasn't the only thing in his new paraplegic life but it was the key to much of his behaviour. He couldn't win without hanging onto it. Only at the moment he did win might there be a chance that, then, he could let go of that despair – and look forward with hope. He was certainly not typical of most patients in similar circumstances. But then I think he was not typical of many things.

Andrew McEwen, a perceptive man, had already been

through the bumpy experience of accompanying Philip to the States. Philip was in a great deal of pain, Andrew explained with almost saintly tolerance; he had tried drugs, even an implant placed near his spine that gave electrical shocks to divert the nerve sensations. He used drink, often, to counter pain. That meant he would frequently be in a condition where his normal behaviour, at best quite aggressive, would be exaggerated by alcohol. Heaving and manipulating him on and off aircraft, dealing with his bodily functions, were all tasks that Andrew tackled uncomplainingly – smiling encouragingly at other members of the public, some of them in a little shock because of the language or the behaviour of the hero in the wheelchair. When Philip flew back to Dayton with Vanessa, he was also accompanied by Andrew and Graham Wood, merrily snapping pictures, cheerfully making jokes. We had arranged to join them later, our size of team could just not afford to wait around for weeks of training and exercising – we were as always on a tight budget. We arrived with about a week to go before they were going to try and make Philip 'walk'. He would be suspended in a safety harness, clutching parallel bars, his legs braced to heavy mid-calf boots. Scores of wires would trail from sensors placed on his nerves and muscles, a computer, half the size of a milk float, would send electrical signals down the wires at carefully programmed intervals, to 'jerk' the legs into a walking motion. A clumsy, flopping 'walking' but still a miracle of achievement, a giant step in the literal sense.

Philip had put on weight, grown a moustache, could now pedal a training bicycle and perform many other muscular functions usually beyond even the ambition of most people in wheelchairs. The improvement in his whole body tone had also made a spectacular difference to his health in general and the condition of his heart, lungs, kidneys and liver. As he had certainly not given up his liking for beer and whisky, I suspect his liver improvement was comparative rather than complete. We arrived ready to film what was intended to be the climax of the film; we filled in some extra scenes with marvellous sequences of Philip working at the local Police Academy as a guest instructor. He had contacted them out of interest and they had taken to him out of a genuine desire to learn from this hero of a police force that didn't automatically equip its officers with guns. All this had taken six months. Living in a motel, confined to one room, the only escape for him, and Vanessa, was when they were asked out by the many new friends they had made in the Dayton Police Department. I found Andrew McEwen and Graham Wood very nearly as 'stir happy' with the working claustrophobia of being on the same assignment for nearly a year. Both of them had managed to return home to Britain for short trips, and Graham had been sent off on other photographic stories, but by the time we checked in – breezy and ready to start shooting – they were as exhausted and drawn out by the waiting as Philip himself was.

The medical specialists attached to Petrofsky's programme were insistent that no test patient could try their system until he or she had passed the fullest medical checks, including careful, full length X-rays of the leg bones. After just a short while without use bones become so brittle that even if the new system got Philip on his feet and 'walking' that could shatter his bones in many places. Wasted muscles had to be restored to their previous tone and leg bones had to be strong again before anyone dared attempt to 'send' the electrical message to the nerves that could produce the action of walking. Because such patients have no feelings of pain in their legs there was also the danger that damage, even burning, could take place without the guinea pig knowing it and before Petrofsky's team could prevent it.

Thus the 'long bone' X-rays due to take place a few days after we arrived, and without which Petrofsky's team wouldn't sanction Philip's walking attempt, were vital to the climax of our documentary. And the results were not good. They showed what could have been a hairline fracture, perhaps the result of his training on the other machines, which would undoubtedly collapse under the strain of trying to stand and 'walk' on the leg. The medical specialists vetoed the attempt. Philip was almost suicidal with depression. Much whisky was consumed that night, and Andrew and I looked at each other wondering how much longer this story was going to go on, how much more *The Daily Mail*, paying all Philip's hotel and travelling expenses, and the BBC, paying out for a whole team to stand by on expenses in the States, would continue to support the cost of the operation.

Philip was persuaded to go on training and wait until the fracture had healed or the X-ray had proved to be a fuzzy picture. He was consumed by disappointment. But, privately, Professor Petrofsky told me: 'What we can achieve is *not* a cure, it would be totally wrong for anybody to get that impression. It's a band-aid, nothing more, an electronic band-aid, a bridge to keep the body going until, perhaps one day, a real cure can be found. It's proper name is a neuro-prosthetic aid and all it really is, is a device to aid the nervous system and improve the body tone and the patient's lifestyle, while we wait for a real cure. It clearly has strong psychological benefits for most patients, allowing them – however briefly – the dignity and satisfaction of being able to stand, move around upright, even if only for a short while.'

As Vanessa told us: 'Our dream was that Philip would go back "walking", but that is clearly not going to happen. He's going through hell at the moment because he'd set his heart on doing that. But he will get over it – and he will "walk", one day. He is determined to be upright, it means more to him than it might to many other people in wheelchairs, and I don't blame him. He's a handsome man and he looks good standing up.' Philip continued to be gloomy, talked often of suicide. But he calmed eventually. *The Daily Mail* found more money to allow him to stay, the Metropolitan Police extended his – and Vanessa's – leave, and the BBC agreed that we should return when the 'fracture' had healed and he was ready to make the attempt. The race was still on, for Philip the chance – however temporary and insecure – to leave his hated 'pram' was still a possibility. We had been through some stormy scenes with him, including the one in which Alex McCall had, in temper, banged his wheelchair against the lavatory wall because of the way he was slagging off his patient and loving, fiancée. But the day before we were due to fly back to Britain (and stand by to return at short notice) Philip seemed in a much calmer mood. I asked him if it meant that he was now going to be able to come to terms with his wheelchair. Yes, by all means feel the reward of being able for a short time to leave his chair, but in the long term accept that he was going to have to live his life in, or at least based on, his wheelchair, accept it for the tool it was, find his peace beyond its confines. He knew perfectly well that I also meant, would he then be able to come to terms with his paralysis, cease the consuming rage which was both driving him – and threatening to destroy him? He blocked me, with that glance from a lowered head that I was beginning to recognise, part mischief and small boy, part clever adult, manipulating others.

'You know, they don't pick people to go into that laboratory unless they have a certain attitude towards the wheelchair. I don't think they take people who will cheerfully say – "Oh well, I'm in a wheelchair for the rest of my life, that's all there is to it" – and then carry on. They don't want people like that, they want fighters. They need fighters because not only do they need their experiments to work, not that they're going to try to fudge anything, but they need the data, they need a positive attitude from everybody. As they say in this country [USA], they need people with balls.' He enjoyed saying that, enjoyed my glance at the cameraman and Alex – he knew swear words were the things most often complained about by viewers (I had often told him so) and that we saw it as no part of our cause or campaign to try and push back some unnecessary boundaries by shocking viewers with more rough language than we need. I grinned:

'Didn't work. That word can probably transmit, they're still your balls – and not my problem.'

They had been in Dayton for six months, they faced up to three months more. We were returning to Britain, to stand by to come out again as soon as Philip was given the all-clear for his attempted 'walk'. I had, in fact, been drafted, rather against my will, to act as one of the Presenters on the BBC's new replacement for *Nationwide,* called *Sixty Minutes.* Although

I had asked if I could be 'excused boots' on this one, the Controller of BBC 1, Alan Hart, had taken the view that, if I didn't co-operate, there would be a lack of goodwill and money for future *Visits*. But if I did do a stint, then he would keep *The Visit* team intact and let me return to them after six months or so. I accepted, with not very good grace I'm afraid, as I had little confidence in the programme, and would rather have been making documentaries. Now I was going back to London to learn how to handle the BBC's complicated new computer systems – yet another recipe for disaster on air, I reflected gloomily.

It was Philip who cheered us all up. My *Visit* colleagues were worried about how we'd manage to keep up the output while I was being a poor man's Cliff Michelmore on the BBC's umpteenth attempt to re-invent the wheel. I told him I knew he was depressed and would feel let down but that I was sure his determination would bring him through in the end.

Generously, he told me not to feel depressed about what I was returning to, said not to worry about him: 'I have the same feeling about succeeding as I had before. I bloody well will walk, there's no doubt about it. I will do it and I know I will do it. It may not be something that will work for the rest of the world but I'll make it work for me. I promised too many people, I promised myself. So I must. This wheelchair, this thing, it's just a rather inconvenient way of getting me around, I've come to feel it's no more than that now.'

'Marvellous, but why has it been important to you to make this film in such a self-revealing way, because I know that you have done that quite deliberately?'

'First I've felt that I wanted to create awareness among people who are not disabled about what it feels like to be robbed when you suddenly are paralysed. It's the robbery of your senses, the robbery of your dignity, you're paralysed and humiliated. Secondly it's been the Year of the Disabled and I wanted to do it then, but during that time I sort of became Cripple of the Year, thanks largely to people like you,' I winced and he went on: 'I didn't enjoy that very much but as a lot of people identified with me and the difficulties I was going through I wanted to prove to them – and the able-bodied – that we have a right in Britain to hope. I just wanted to give people hope.' I felt humble and small as I shook the hand of this volatile man, who could swing between moods so violently, who knew so much more than any of us who had never known what it is like to be sentenced to life in a wheel-chair, to live in pain and frustration.

I flew home ahead of Alex and Jan and the crew and 'signed on' at the BBC's Lime Grove, wondering how many *Visit* films I could have made with the huge sums of money which had already been spent on sixty-five new computers for the pro-gramme.

We had been on the air with *Sixty Minutes* for nearly three months and Christmas was approaching, when we received word from Dayton that Philip was ready to walk. I begged them to time it for a weekend when *Sixty Minutes* wasn't on the air, swapped two shifts with Nick Ross and headed for Heathrow. It was blowing a blizzard when I arrived, still wearing the lightweight suit I had just presented a programme in. Jan and Alex were already there, the walk was timed for Saturday.

The medics had pronounced him fit, he was smiling and relaxed, Vanessa looked tense, her eyes shadowed and dark. Andrew McEwen was ready, Graham Wood was cooing over some expensive new piece of flash equipment. It was 8 a.m. on Saturday and Jerry Petrofsky was bulked over his computer keyboard, Philip was wired, harnessed – and ready.

And he did it. Five crude, clumsy steps. Marvellous steps, miracle steps. The look on his face as we filmed his personal victory gleamed with pride and emotion. He stood, grinning like a man on top of Everest, 5 foot 10 inches tall again. 'Oh, it felt good. It really did, Desmond.'

And the wheelchair? 'It doesn't mean a thing to me now. Beforehand I hated it, despised it because I thought I had become part of it. But now I know it's nothing, just a con-venience. I've beaten it. I've won – I did win, didn't I?'

'Yes Philip, you certainly did win.'

And he went on during the next few days to walk more. More than fifty steps.

The plane connecting me with a flight back to England, and *Sixty Minutes*, was late because of snowstorms and blizzards. The connection time at Chicago had always been desperately short. I was due on the air on Monday evening – I had hoped to fly back for Sunday night. The crew of the aircraft bringing me in to Chicago were magnificent, they radioed ahead to the British Airways departure gate, they rushed me first out of the plane and into an airport maintenance vehicle, waiting on the ground. It skidded and slushed its way across one of the world's largest airports, Chicago's O'Hare, and arrived at the plane just as they were shutting the door. The driver and I ran up the steps beneath the Jetway and banged on the door, inches only from the face of the steward who was locking it. He shrugged – and turned away. The plane took off and I spent the night in a motel attached to a Greek restaurant, on the highway about thirty miles away from the airport. I knew I would have only about one hour in bed and then have to start back to catch the plane home in the morning. I spent most of that hour phoning Esther and asking her to phone, in turn, David Lloyd, the editor of *Sixty Minutes*, and let him know that I would be back on the Monday morning and could he get one of the other presenters to cover for me. She rang back to say that he would rather I went from the airport straight to the office and performed my shift, and went on air – and so I did. Subsequently, I left *Sixty Minutes* to return, gratefully, full time to *The Visit*. Shortly after that, the programme left the screen forever – another television experiment that had not worked.

The Philip Olds story was told in two programmes which we sub-titled, 'The Rage' and 'Get Up and Walk'. We all felt that it was a story we would have to revisit. But before we did I found myself at the centre of an astonishing row in the medical establishment. Leading orthopaedic specialists, and many of the distinguished men and women who run Stoke Mandeville Hospital, felt that we had been irresponsible. They argued that all medical attention should be devoted to making the paralysed patient come to terms with his disability, accept and make the best of his wheelchair – and not be encouraged with what they called false hope, even falsely giving people the idea that Philip had found a cure. I read vitriolic attacks on *The Visit* in the charity publications, attacks which inevitably found their way into the national press.

I felt, with the BBC, that in fact, we had all behaved responsibly, and decided that we shouldn't engage in a noisy dog fight, but only respond when questioned. So, when asked, I replied that we thought that not all people would initially accept their paralysis or their wheelchairs as calmly as doctors wanted, that the world of wheelchair-users – millions of them – had many people and many attitudes. Some of them wanted to walk and stand, however briefly and clumsily, and their determination to achieve this didn't make them view their future through rose-tinted spectacles. Rather, they were men and women to be admired for their spirit and honesty – certainly there was nothing distorting or improper about a documentary team following such a pioneering case. The level of vehemence exhibited by some orthopaedic consultants still surprised me but we turned our attention to making other programmes. And two years later we started to make the third film about Philip, 'Marching Forward'.

By that time an extraordinary and valuable charity had sprung into being, in the wake of *The Daily Mail* stories and our broadcasts. The WALK fund (short for Walk Again Limb Kinetics fund, and originally called The Philip Olds Trust) was started by the generous reaction and donations from thousands of readers and viewers. In a disused ward at St Vincent's Hospital, at Stanmore, London, they had set up a training and fitting service for the paralysed – preparing them to walk. Half a dozen young people were already working there, more were joining every week. The key to this huge leap forward was twofold; the discovery of a marvellous brace made by a London genius, Roy Douglas, and the miniaturisation of the computer controls and sensors. In New Orleans, Louisiana, Roy Douglas had perfected a full body brace that worked superbly with the newly miniaturised computers developed by Jerry Petrofsky, in Dayton. It meant that patients could carry the computer and power pack in a small skier's bag and, wearing the brace and special underwear fitted with the sensors, and using a walking frame with trigger controls on the handles, they could 'fire' electricity into their dead muscles – and walk. They could even dance. At Dayton we saw Philip walk up and down a corridor, watched others, ahead of him in development in the programme, walking around the university campus, riding bicycles, climbing stairs. In New Orleans we watched children, using only the brace, running into toy shops, one of them climbing trees, another even water-skied. These were children whose parents had been told they would be confined to wheelchairs, or even to bed, for the rest of their lives, victims of conditions like muscular dystrophy, spina bifida and other deteriorating diseases. Their parents now regarded the future in a different light – and the children were able to join in the world of normal education and play.

I asked Philip whether he felt rage and resentment about his wheelchair now: 'I sometimes forget where I've left it, it no longer is my prison – just a tool. I know perfectly well I'm always going to need it. What's happening to me isn't a cure, but I still think it's a miracle. I've changed in myself now, I'm calmer, more relaxed, far less bitter about life – more sober in my conduct.'

Philip was still serving in the Metropolitan Police, working as an instructor in the Police College at Hendon; he had become fond of the job and the sight of him wheeling himself around the campus was a familiar one to all the students. Few police recruits can have failed to know why he was in a wheelchair and few can have failed to reflect, thoughtfully, on the fact that he had been acting in the line of duty, as a policeman, when he was gunned down and left paralysed for life. The 'Met' had given him more leave to fly to the United States to take part in the latest developments. He had already been a number of times to the WALK fund ward in St Vincent's, but he had never before seen the children at Roy Douglas's clinic literally, running around. He told me:

'It's a wonderful kick to know that half a million people, including kids, particularly the kids, suffering from spina bifida, cerebral palsy and paraplegics like me can now benefit from what I've done with those first few strides. We've come a long way since and we're certainly no longer pathetic, are we? And, what's more, we haven't even started yet, that's the marvellous thing.'

Andrew McEwen, who by now was a senior trustee and very much a driving force in the WALK fund, and who also accompanied us on this trip, for *The Daily Mail*, told me: 'I honestly think it's time now to stop taking away hope from newly injured people. People with new spinal cord injuries should no longer be told that there is no hope and that they will never walk again, that they must condition themselves to life in a wheelchair. That is no longer true. The whole medical philosophy must change. Nobody has found a cure for the injuries or diseases that put these people in wheelchairs but we have found a way to get people out of them, if they want. The improvement in general fitness is saving the National Health Service millions of pounds a year. By combining the work of Roy Douglas and Jerry Petrofsky we now have something that's both practical and can be offered to people in Britain immediately, we've compacted fifteen years' research into the last two years. Our job now is to speed public acceptance, *and* medical acceptance, of this system and to make the medical community be prepared to try it out in their hospitals and allow this achievement to become public property through the National Health Service. The most exciting thing is to discover that the brace can be used, without the stimulation system, to treat all sorts of other conditions. We thought we were dealing with half a million paraplegics in America and maybe 50 000 in Britain – but now we can reach, and help, literally millions more people.'

We stopped to go back to our motel and change for a party. At the university all Petrofsky's guinea pigs were celebrating with food and drink and music and dancing – and the wheelchairs would be parked in the hall outside. And Andrew, normally a shy and reserved man, made a speech. 'Two and a half years ago nearly everybody in this room (there were about sixty people present) was in a wheelchair. Now I look around and see you standing, walking and even dancing. And that's wonderful. What you've shown here is that for hundreds and thousands of people around the world there is hope and in fact the practicality that one can get up out of a wheelchair and walk. Philip came here in a wheelchair with wasted legs, perhaps half the weight he is now – and with hope, not much else. He goes back with a practical walking system and that gives all of us in London more pleasure than we can begin to describe.'

The next morning I went to the flat that Vanessa and Philip had been loaned for their stay. She was reading a magazine, he was standing in the kitchenette, reaching into the high cupboard for mugs in order to make us all coffee. It was a remarkable sight – and he knew it, and revelled in it. So did we.

They flew back to London later that day and Philip was photographed by *The Daily Mail*, and filmed by us leaving the plane, upright and standing on the top of the steps, waving to the small, cheering crowd – waving, for all the world to see, at his cheerful future. That's how we ended the third programme.

Soon after that, several National Health hospitals started supplying and fitting the same kind of braces, and at least three of them began to develop the fitting and supplying of the electrical stimulation system. The WALK fund had by then asked me to serve as a Trustee, as they had also Assistant Commissioner Hugh Annesley of the Metropolitan Police. Gradually dozens of people came forward to be fitted and trained in the use of the brace. More general use of electrical stimulation was delayed by the discovery that moisture penetrated the wiring of pace-makers. This meant that the Febrile Electrical Stimulation (FES) system was vulnerable to the same fault – and it had hundreds of wires. It is still being modified but few people doubt that it won't be long before it is made workable and becomes part of everyday life for those paraplegics who want to try it. But, so far, more than 200 patients have been fitted with the brace, at St Vincent's, many of them children.

In March 1985 Philip and Vanessa had announced their official engagement; she proudly wore his diamond solitaire ring during the whole time we were filming. But in November, at about the time we transmitted the final programme in this remarkable trilogy, they announced that they were postponing the wedding for a year. Philip had been previously married and the reason they gave was that they both had too many things to organise in the next few months. In fact, life had been difficult between them both for some months; the strain of their long and complicated relationship was beginning to tell. Vanessa decided she needed time and distance to assess the situation. She had been living with Philip in his bungalow for the past three years but now she went back to her own flat, still seeing him nearly every day. Philip became more and more broody, felt let down and started to return to his old black moods of depression. But I had seen many couples overcome worse, and there was never any doubting Vanessa's love and devotion to Philip. The only problem was: could this intelligent and passionate girl and this bright and fiery man manage to settle down together without their married life being one long row? Vanessa became ill, very ill. She had to go into hospital to have an enormous tumour removed, fortunately with no permanent damage or effect.

In August 1986 Philip was still living alone, but visited almost daily by Vanessa. He made headlines again when he accidentally shot a friend, commodity broker Russell Dalton, in the shoulder, because a single-barrelled shotgun, he kept in bed with him, went off. The friend was rushed to hospital, and made it quite clear that it had been an accident. Philip said that he kept the gun near him because he lived alone and felt he needed it for his protection. I spoke to him on the phone and suggested that what he'd done was daft, to say the least. He agreed and promised 'Don't worry, Desmond, I'm not going to do anything silly again. It was a stupid accident, my fault. But I'm grown up now.' I wasn't entirely reassured.

Some weeks later, I met Vanessa, looking more glamorous

than ever, in her police sergeant's uniform: quite coincidentally, she was on duty when Esther and I were lucky enough to be invited, with the children, to be in the Royal box at the Horse of The Year show at Wembley. From among the line of police keeping an eye on the crowd, she called my name and, with a nod of approval from the inspector on duty, ran forward to give me a huge hug and a kiss. I was pleased to see her looking so fit and well and promised to slip out in an interval to catch up on the news. The Princess Royal, Princess Anne, turned to me with that famous grin, as I hurriedly caught up with the party, 'You seem to get on well with police officers,' she said.

In October 1986 Philip and Vanessa spent the evening in his bungalow, planning their future together, when an argument blew up. It wasn't unusual, indeed it was a common occurrence. Vanessa went home to her own flat, as she most frequently did. They had been through a three-month trial separation earlier in the year but now they were trying to make a 'go' of it again. That evening, Philip had already drunk a considerable amount, he was broody and quarrelsome, a mood most of us knew well, the old Philip, the Philip of the wheelchair, before he walked. He still used his brace regularly, still visited the WALK fund patients in Stanmore, but his failure to 'behave' calmly with Vanessa was weighing him down. He seemed unable to avoid picking fights and he was clearly unable to consider a future without her.

With Vanessa gone for the night, he took quantities of pain-killers, sleeping pills and tranquillisers. He had already consumed enough liquor to be four times over the legal level for driving. The next day a neighbour found him dead. He had fallen from his bed. Scrawled on the sheet, in ball point ink, were the words: 'Sorry 'Vessa'.

At the inquest, nearly two months later, the Coroner recorded an open verdict, commenting that the high level of alcohol in his blood may have confused him enough not to realise how many drugs he had taken, nor the implications of what he had done. At his funeral, Vanessa placed a single red rose on his coffin. His colleagues and friends, and his many admirers in the police force came to honour the man who had shown nothing but courage and strength, in their eyes.

Questioned by the Police Federation, later, the Home Secretary at the time, Douglas Hurd, assured them that the gunman who had shot Philip, Stuart Blackstock, sentenced to life imprisonment for wounding with intent to evade arrest, but able to be considered for release after serving only a third of the time, would not leave prison for at least twenty years – 'If I have anything to do with it.' Several senior policemen commented publicly that Philip Olds's death was murder, as surely as if he had been killed that evening when he drew his truncheon to try and stop a raid on an off-licence – and was shot.

As if all that was not depressing enough as an end to a life, I was slightly dismayed by the comments of some of the leaders of charities and organisations for the spinal injured. Two of these were Stephen Bradshaw of the Spinal Injuries Association, who condemned the way he says Philip was 'handled' by the media. And Mary Ann Tyrrell, also of the Spinal Injuries Association, who wrote to *The Guardian* accusing the press and TV of creating the impression that a cure was just around the corner, and saying that this 'media hype' of a tragic case had led to an even more tragic outcome. She pointed out that for most paralysed people the loss of bowel and bladder function, and the sexual dysfunction were as hard to bear as the loss of walking, and the media had been responsible for raising false hopes. Alex Scott, the brilliant and talented film cameraman from BBC Scotland, who had filmed much of Philip's story with us, told me: 'She's wrong – and I know why.'

A few years ago, Alex had had a colostomy operation and since then has returned to a full and active life, proof that a man of spirit and courage can overcome the difficult-to-accept fact that one's bowel function has ceased to operate normally. He told me: 'I could hardly continue to work as a cameraman, travel round the world with people like you, do initial training of guide dogs for the blind, as I do in my spare time, if I had –

instead – lost the use of my legs.' He was right, from his point of view. There will always be many different reactions. Mary Ann Tyrrell may well be right, but limited in her point of view (and I found her attack a little tasteless coming, as it did, so close to the funeral). Can she not see that Philip Olds was right, from his point of view, too?

A few weeks ago, Vanessa, Andrew McEwen, Jan Riddell, Alex McCall and I met for dinner. Vanessa looked in blooming health, tall, luscious-haired, a thirty-five-year-old beauty, to turn the heads of every man in the restaurant. She was still wearing Philip's engagement ring. She caught my look. 'I can't take it off,' she told me. 'Maybe someday, but Philip will always be in my heart and if there is ever to be anyone else – and I'm getting on a bit now to that age where you always find that all the good ones of your own age are already married – then that person will have to know that there will always be a special part of me that belongs to Philip. That's not to say I can't, and won't, love anyone else, I'm sure I will – but whoever it is will have to understand about Philip.'

She has been through two serious operations and is now fully recovered but it was obvious that Philip's death and the emotionally exhausting aftermath had taken its toll. Now she was in fine spirits. Her job at Wembley police station was giving her great satisfaction – 'I really love it, absolutely love it.' She went back recently to the Dayton Police Academy, to give them Philip's most treasured police possession, his helmet from his days as a motor-cycle policeman; Hendon Police College already have his medals in the impressive collection there. 'In Dayton they made a little ceremony at the time for the widows of their own policeman who had been killed on duty and they included me to be "honoured" as Philip's widow. I've kept his other things, they don't give me pain, only happy memories. But he's still very much part of my life, maybe too much so.'

For that reason, perhaps, Vanessa is writing a book, an account of her years with Philip and their joint struggle (without her partnership there is no doubt that he couldn't have done it) to get him walking and upright. She is producing the book with journalist Maureen Owen. She intends to call it *Sorry 'Vessa*. 'That', she told us, 'says it all for me, sums up our relationship, sums up the best of Philip. I don't think anybody really knows how wonderful he was, they often saw the irritable and the black side of him but he really was a remarkable man, for me nobody has yet matched up to him.

'I have no regrets about any of it. From that very first moment that I set eyes on him, he was the only man for me. His determination to walk was certainly not the reason that made him die. That didn't unsettle him. He loved it, I loved it. We used to go to St Vincent's and watch the others training there and it gave him great pleasure, but most of all watching the children, that was really wonderful. Just think of the good things that have followed in his footsteps, and I do mean footsteps.

'I can never be sure that what he did that last night was to kill himself – I think he may have been confused by drink and not known how many pills he was taking. And scribbling "Sorry 'Vessa," on the sheet was fairly typical – it could have been a message for me when I came back in the morning, as he knew I would, and discovered the mess.' She saw our thoughtful expressions. 'I don't know, I just don't know.

'That's why I have to finish the book. Then I'll be able to close that chapter of my life, properly. Then I'll be able to find some peace and settle the guilt in me. Oh yes, there's guilt. I wasn't there to stop it, was I? But if I had thought he was going to do anything silly I would never have left, I never did before, always stayed if he was being difficult. This time it seemed all right to leave, he seemed to be all right – I thought he'd go to sleep and we'd see each other in the morning ... but I'm not depressed any more. I have been left nothing but marvellous memories, many of them.'

I hope Vanessa's book is a huge success, she deserves it. I hope, when it's finished, that, then, her restless heart can be still – and her life go on in peace.

CHAPTER EIGHT

PAT MUMMY –
THE RELUCTANT HEROINE

The advertising men in their Katherine Hamnett suits, charged with creating and fostering a new commercial image for British Airways, came up with the commercial seen by millions – the smiling British Airways stewardess (or steward) who sorts out a traffic jam, recovers a lost briefcase, helps an old lady, charms a businessman and understands a young girl. The short, brilliantly made films, which all end with the steward or stewardess taking off with arms spread rather like Superman, charmed viewers all over the world, and sold the new, caring image of an airline fighting off its old reputation for snooty insensitivity. Each of these commercials cost more to make than several full-length *Visit* films. And in my humble and prejudiced view, all of them together didn't do as much for the airline as the story we told of one real-life, golden-haired stewardess, Pat Kerr, and her personal kind of caring and dedication. She became an example that inspired the whole of the airline staff and changed the lives of hundreds of children in a Bangladesh orphanage. We started telling her story, almost from the beginning – it became, in the end, three films spread over nearly four years.

For eleven years Pat used her skill and charm to comfort passengers flying round the world at 35 000 feet. In between these long-haul trips she and the rest of the crew frequently had several days to spend, waiting for the next flight, usually in a comfortable hotel, most often relaxing by the pool or enjoying the local sights. On the regular trip to Dhaka, capital of the poorest of the Third World countries, the 'stop-over' was no exception. But Pat was. She was invited by a friend she'd met out there to visit a back-street orphanage, run by a struggling Canadian charity, Families for Children. Four hundred children, half naked, were crowded into an old factory building, aged from a few hours old to sixteen years. They slept, huddled together, as many as thirty at a time on wooden platforms. They ate one main meal a day. They wore no shoes and just one shirt-like garment, taken from a common pile at the beginning of each day. They had no individual possessions, not even a particular space to call their own. Many of the babies were ill, quite a few died. The sanitation was virtually non-existent. The staff, of Western volunteers and Bengali helpers, were caring but overworked. And yet the place was filled with love and laughter and smiling faces. And outside, on the streets from which so many of them had been rescued, these children would have fared worse, no food, no shelter. The young ones would have died, the survivors would have begged. Just beyond the crumbling walls of the orphanage, in the teeming, sweltering streets, lay the constant reminder – of how lucky, by comparison, these children were.

Pat joined in, became a helper. More than that, she persuaded, first the members of her own crew, and gradually many others also, to help. Gradually the Dhaka orphanage became the airline staff project, they borrowed an office at Heathrow, from their bosses, to run a fund-raising campaign, they collected clothing, medicines, toys, toilet equipment, milk bottles, baby's potties. The generously conniving airline turned a blind eye when black plastic bags full of supplies, just marked simply 'The Orphanage', would be handed over at check-in desks, or passed through cargo handling. (One Christmas I drove to Heathrow with three huge bags of hardly used children's clothing and a British Airways crew entering the building spotted what I was carrying and took it off me to hand in.) On stop-overs in Dhaka, Flight Captains would spend their three days digging drains; engineers ran a scheme making cots for the babies with welding equipment and metal piping; stewardesses cared for sick children, cuddled and played with the well ones, put all their airline training and skills to work. For eight years, since the revolution and the new government in Bangladesh, adoptions of Bengali children by Westerners, had not been allowed because of the fierce strictures of Islamic

law. So the staff of British Airways adopted the whole orphanage. . . .

And then the children and the helpers were issued with
eviction notices. The owner of the building wanted it back, he
was tolerant and understanding, prepared to wait a while –
but not too long. It could have been the last straw, finished
the place off altogether. Pat and her colleagues went into high
gear. They decided to build a new orphanage, a children's
village, able to house not 400 children but 600. They were
given the help of Godfrey Crook, British Airways property
services manager; they found designers, architects. They
hunted in Bangladesh for land, a nearly impossible task in one
of the most overcrowded countries in the world (the whole
nation is about the size of Wales, has a population as big as
the United States and is, all too frequently, two thirds under
water).

The fund-raising became almost frenetic in its pace, pan-
tomimes, collecting boxes, even a sponsored shoe shine at
British airports. On this last one Jan, Alex and I joined in,
complete with posters, at Glasgow airport. We blackmailed
passengers into paying as high as £10 for a shine, one man,
fresh from duty on an oil rig, gave £50. Alex inadvertently tore
the buckle off one businessman's Gucci shoe, Jan managed to
cover a pair of white socks with black polish. And I found
myself face to face with the BBC's Controller for Scotland, the
impressive figure of Pat Chalmers. With a grin he pointed out
that he'd always wanted me on my knees before him – and
gave me a good Scottish £10 note, in return for a polish.

They needed at least £800 000 – an almost impossible dream.
They needed the help of the Bangladeshi government, the aid
of local builders, the continued support of the airline staff.
They already had the unstinted admiration of Sandra Simpson,
the remarkable Canadian woman who had founded Families
for Children and who herself had personally adopted an astonishing family of twenty-seven children from Third World countries. Nobody knew better how difficult it was to raise funds
and then how complicated it could be putting them to good
use in poor countries. They had found a piece of land – at

fifteen feet above sea level it was practically a mountain by Bangladeshi standards – certainly above the level of the flood waters that so regularly devastate this country. There was no road, just a cratered and torn-up track between rice fields; no electricity, but they started considering a generator; it was more than thirty miles from Dhaka – they would have to keep a small reception centre going in the city before ferrying the children to the country. But it was the country, better smells, better sights, a better life. Sandra Simpson immediately started planning a fish farm which would not only supply the children with a valuable source of protein, but act as an income to defray the costs of running this new, huge project. They were granted an audience by President Ershad – who promised them all the support he could.

During all this time we had been filming in Britain and Bangladesh, travelling on low fares – with the help of an understanding British Airways – backwards and forwards with the Tri-star fleet that operates on that route. The director of cabin services for the Tri-star operation was a charming and persuasive Irishman, Gerry Devereux. Not only did he fully back the efforts of his crews, he joined in with vigour. As workers they were an example to the world; as an executive, Gerry was an example to top management. And Pat, who had started the whole thing, tried modestly to avoid the limelight at every step. But that could never have worked. She was awarded the Unsung Hero Award, presented by Prince Michael of Kent. She was given many periods of extended leave of absence by the airline, used all her travel concessions to return to the orphanage at every opportunity. At one point she contracted dysentery and became seriously ill.

She is a smiling, laughing-eyed, beautiful person. She and I got on like a house on fire – 'You're just a sucker for thin blondes with big teeth and a smile,' she joked. I think she's right. . . . She is the much-loved daughter of slightly bemused parents who live in idyllic surroundings in Lostwithiel, Cornwall. Her sister is married with children and her parents worry that this single-minded dedication to a cause is exhausting Pat and ruining her health, and that means that Pat is missing the opportunity of a personal family life. But Pat has no regrets, doesn't see it in those terms. There is much wisdom, much of it harshly learned, in her by now. She is a believing person but ask her, as I did, if she believes in God. And she'll answer, not any more.

'If there is a God then he isn't doing a very good job at the moment,' she told me. 'When you hold little babies, as they die, it's difficult to find consolation in the thought that it must be God's will.' It had been the end of a long day at the orphanage, there had been two admissions, both tragic. One, a teenage mother with a baby to leave because the rickshaw-bicyclist father had been killed by a lorry the night before; the other a mother of two children, who earned her living begging on the streets and slept in a doorway, and who felt she could care for the baby, still being breast-fed, but would have to leave the eighteen-month-old little girl behind. The people of Bangladesh are among the most beautiful and gentle I have ever met, in half a lifetime of travelling round the world, but life in Bangladesh is impossibly cruel, almost too painful to consider. In a burst of insensitivity, diplomat Henry Kissinger once described Bangladesh as 'The basket case of the Third World'. That, from an American, escorting film stars to Washington parties and shuttling first class between capital cities, hardly struck me as tactful, to say the least.

The Princess Royal, Princess Anne, on one of her inspiring and fatiguing Save The Children tours, visited the orphanage and talked for a long time to Pat. Stories were appearing in the national press at home and we went on filming at intervals. We became a familiar part of the orphanage, we became used to the children's habits. They live in a huge gregarious group but what they lack is personal contact. They are loving and tactile, never shy, always generous. Not one of us could ever move without two or three children hung round our necks, literally, and several more trailing along holding onto our hands or clutching at our clothing. They carried all the equipment, they never stole a thing, they loved having their pictures taken, loved being cuddled even more. That way you get to know, very well indeed, at least the two or three that cling closest to your face. That way I fell in love with Hiramoti, seven years old (but looking little more than four) huge-eyed, impish.

I still write to her, not enough, and send her photographs of my own children. She had been in the orphanage nearly all her life, had an uncle somewhere, they thought. I tried to adopt her – and nearly got arrested. Islamic law says that children can only be adopted by a relative, and should be. Tell that to a child abandoned on a river bank, only a few days old. I telephoned home, it took hours to get through.

'Hi, the children in the orphanage are wonderful and I've got this funny desire I ought to talk over with you . . .'

'Bring as many as you want, any age. We'll love them as much as you do,' said Esther before I could even begin to explain.

But I wasn't allowed to. When we interviewed the President, surrounded by his bodyguards in the palace, I raised the issue after we'd finished filming – what better time? His face became stern and the more I persisted, explaining that there was a large Bangladeshi community in London and I would love to bring a child up in the Islamic faith and with an awareness of Bengali culture, his face became sterner and he made restless movements. The British Ambassador was there, we had been showing the new architect's plans to the President, and he stepped in and led me to one side.

'When they put people in prison in this country, old boy,' he told me, 'it can take me a very long time to get them out. I shouldn't push your luck, there hasn't been an adoption out of this country for eight years now, it's as much to do with national pride as it is to do with Islamic law.'

I took his advice and drifted back to talk to the President about more general matters. The President (a graduate of Sandhurst Military Academy in England, an experienced general with a reputation for throwing opponents in gaol) told me they were about to have free elections in his country. With my mind still on Hiramoti and with the words of the Ambassador still in my ears, I unthinkingly said: 'Oh, are you going to let the leaders of the opposition party out of prison then?' There was a completely frozen moment, time enough for me to contemplate my whole previous life – and my short and dismal future. Then there was a gentle, but very slight and somewhat wintry smile as he gazed thoughtfully at me. 'I so enjoy what you are doing with this film for the children of my country,' he murmured quietly, shook hands, salaamed to the room – and left. I couldn't quite meet Alex McCall's eye. He made his views felt in the mini-bus on the way back to our two-star horror of a hotel, as we bounced about on top of our filming equipment. He can be very, very Glaswegian, when he's roused. 'Bloody idjit, get us all locked up at worst, or thrown out at least,' he said. 'You should know better, let's have a drink and toast your freedom. Anyway, have you thought of kidnap?'

Hiramoti is still there, nearly twelve now, and I see her whenever I can route myself through the country. I write and she writes back, sending little drawings signed 'Hiramoti loves Desmond.' She's a little shy now, growing into womanhood, and so far we've all taken care to ensure that she doesn't know that we tried to adopt her, doesn't feel any more abandoned or rejected than life has made her feel in the first place.

The first documentary became two films, under the title 'Down to Earth', Part 1: 'Pat Mummy' (what all the children called her) and Part 2: 'We'll Take Good Care of You'. At the end of the two broadcasts we asked BBC presentation to put up a notice and make an announcement to the effect that any viewers, interested in knowing more, could contact the people in the orphanage fund – and we gave the address. I now have to confess that this device is a deliberate way of sliding past a BBC rule. It may be frowned on but it still happens, with any number of programmes. But part of the BBC's huge structure is devoted to organising the regular charity appeals. And a programme, rather than an appeal, that generates money for a cause or a charity, can't be stopped but in their view it complicates matters for some good causes which may have been on a waiting list for years. But half the good causes in the country have been the recipients of funds raised as a result of their work being seen in documentaries. Indeed, several wonderful charities have actually sprung into being as the result of some of our *Visit* programmes. The WALK fund, which I mentioned in the last chapter, The Disfigurement Guidance Centre, grew and expanded after 'The Boy David', The Katy Green porphyria Trust, after our film about the little girl who couldn't be exposed to light – and others. For my sins, and to my pleasure, I serve as trustee or advisor to a number of them. With the Dhaka orphanage, the second film left the story, as it was in life, still in the air. Would they make their target, raise enough to rescue the children before they were evicted and thrown back on the streets, from which so many of them had come? The viewers' response was amazing – nearly £200 000 came rolling in after the broadcast. Lord King had promised to pay £1 for every three they raised (up to a limit of £75 000) out of British Airways' funds. They had exceeded £1 million, they had saved the children.

During the next two years they built the place and during that time Pat was given an MBE for her work. We continued to film, knowing that the third programme would have to show the children moving into their new home. We had commissioned audience research, mainly because our Scottish bosses took the view that people didn't want progress reports. I disagreed fundamentally with this, everything I heard on the streets, everything I'd learned in making other programmes, everything I knew from the success of *That's Life* (where they regularly bring viewers up-to-date on their campaigns and causes) proved that viewers actually had a need to be kept informed. Pat Chalmers, on an occasion when we had just received an award for best documentary, rather uncharitably growled at me: 'I gather you're going back over old ground in the next series, rather like eating your own entrails, isn't it?'

However, our decision was proved right: we received higher than ever viewing figures and, as well, a very good appreciation index from the viewers themselves. But being right isn't always the thing that makes you most popular with the boss, which is why, I think, he made no move to stop us being dropped by BBC Scotland when we moved and became an Independent team.

Pat Kerr never liked being the centre of press or media attention but she knew also that the publicity was good for the cause. She did the rounds of raffles, openings, cheque hand-overs, interviews with newspapers, and photo-calls. She claims to have enjoyed being interviewed, by me, about her personal life. 'Fighting you off was good fun.' She wanted not to be a 'personality' but if it helped would have given everything of herself. Her immediate boss, Gerry Devereux, knew what it took out of her. 'She, and the others, have knocked themselves sideways for this cause – but it's also been the best image the airline could have. So many people fly into Third World countries, or fly over them, and never comprehend what conditions are really like. I think the example they've all set is wonderful.'

By this time Pat was doing more work with the orphanage, than in the air. She had always been told that this was never a problem. Indeed, the top man in publicity in British Airways told me that the films we had made around her were probably worth millions of pounds to the airline in terms of publicity. I felt they deserved it. But Pat mightn't have felt so generous when she was sent for by her personnel boss, who wanted to talk about her long-term future, as he described it. 'Let's face it,' he said to Pat, as he looked at her thin face, tired and straight off a flight back from Dhaka, needing no more than a few days' rest to recover her vitality, 'You're no spring chicken any more.' It was then, Pat told me later, that she decided not to stay with the airline.

That boss has since been made redundant himself. But so too has Gerry Devereux, the man who helped and inspired them all. His own job vanished in a reorganisation shuffle. The mainstay of the fund-raising office, Maura, has died of cancer since and the man who planned and supervised the building has also taken early retirement. None of them regret for one moment the hours, the effort they've put in – even the price, it seems, they may have had to pay in terms of their jobs or careers. The cynical may be led to think that fiercely competitive organisations like airlines prefer their staff to get on with the job of serving customers. That, at least, can be measured and assessed – public relations is a funny business and publicity successes inside the ranks of a workforce tend to make top management nervous. Conformity, corporate effort, praise to the boss and pass the cigars are, perhaps, surer ways to please than becoming (even only for a moment) better known than the main image of the business. The fact that the main image of British Airways is one of caring is a fact that can be redefined as caring for British Airways and its customers. But to think the whole airline felt like that would be unfair. Lord King, the Chairman, was tremendously enthusiastic for the Dhaka project, so was Sir Colin Marshall, The Chief Executive. However, they all knew that the image was one thing and the business of an airline is flying business, not charity business, or Third World understanding, or looking after orphans. They had already done more than many airlines would and they understood, as many airlines wouldn't, exactly what motivated their staff in the Dhaka project, and it is still understandably, and rightly, known as the British Airways orphanage.

Finally, we all arrived in Dhaka, and trekked out to Sreepur, the site of the new orphanage, for the official opening. It was finished, they'd moved the children, they'd somehow acquired two hundred more, the grass had been planted but hadn't yet started to grow, the fishpond was planned but not yet dug, the President was coming, by armoured helicopter, Lord King was coming, by well-sprung car. We had been commuting in our battered filming van. (The 3 miles from the road down the approach track took nearly as long to travel as the 30 miles from Dhaka.) I had been walking quietly round the paddy fields with a suddenly rather grown-up Hiramoti. Pat told me that getting the children to move had been difficult, they were really used to an urban setting.

'Initially they didn't really like it, we moved a small group in first, and they started mucking about and climbing on the roofs and generally misbehaving. So I took five of them back to Dhaka with me as a punishment, which was taking a bit of a risk because they didn't necessarily see it as a punishment. But it worked, once I got them back they were really miserable and started telling the others how nice Sreepur was. And after that it was just a damned hard slog. I didn't realise how much we'd grown in size until we started the move. You know we have this policy of never refusing any child in need, admission, so in fact we've moved into this new paradise and it's full at once. But we'll always make room for more. We get on well with all the local people and our teenage boys are learning metal working and woodworking skills and the girls are training as nursing orderlies, and will be able to work in the local hospital.

'The thing that pleases me most,' she went on 'is the fact that all those wonderful people who gave hundreds of thousands of pounds – and mostly in small denominations, like £5 or £10 – will be able to see from your film how their money was spent, what it has done for the children.'

It was the day before the opening ceremony and nearly all the children were running around in the warmth of the evening, without a stitch on. Naked, they had been rehearsing their lining of the Presidential walk-about route; naked, they had waved flags and cheered; naked, they had eaten their evening meal. Tomorrow, all their dresses washed and dried, they would be wearing clothes, looking as smart as they could. They saw nothing unusual in it and I thought of the children I knew – and my own – and the number of clothes they had, and I felt guilt. The people who'd been fund-raising were arriving, Tommy Miah, himself a success story from Bangladesh who now runs a popular restaurant in Edinburgh, had come to cook a giant curry for the hundreds of people who would celebrate in the morning. A group of Canadian parents who had adopted Bangladeshi children, before the present regime stopped it, had brought their children back. It was fascinating watching them make friends with the children they'd left behind in the orphanage as babies, and come to terms with their own culture. They may be Canadians now but they were discovering that they were Bengali too.

And suddenly it was all happening, speeches, helicopters, the President discovering that they had no road or electricity, pledging to provide both, Pat and Sandra Simpson in tears, the children running and waving and cheering – and perhaps a few of them understanding what it was all about.

And I interviewed the President (and Alex held his breath, but I behaved myself), and his helicopter, with its back-up helicopter flew away; and I interviewed Lord King and he motored off, looking pained in anticipation of the harsh and bumpy ride home. And Pat and I sat down under a tree, each of us with a couple of armfuls of children – and Pat told me of her next dream.

'I think the airlines of the world should really stand up and take notice of all this. Because they are the only people who can do a project like this, it costs them very little really. They're flying in and out of the Third World countries all the time. It's cost-effective too because airlines make money out of flying to countries like this; they wouldn't do it if they didn't. I truly believe that all the airlines should get together and become involved in returning something to the countries they travel to. Not just British airlines – we have a pretty good record – but all the airlines of the world. The world is shrinking. Altruism is becoming a survival characteristic and if we don't all start to help each other there won't be anybody left to help. These children, these children here – and how could anybody ever forget them now? – they are the future of this planet – our future.'

Twelve months later, Pat is no longer on the British Airways staff, but she is still on good terms with them, still encouraged by them to travel regularly to Dhaka. She lives in a small, cluttered flat in Chiswick, but spends most of her time working away from home. She has been sponsored by a splendid English couple, who now in live in Germany and were so moved by her work that they have paid for her to continue for at least another year. And after that – 'Something will happen, I don't quite know what, but it always does.

'The charity can't afford to pay me, so I must find a way. You'd never recognise the place now, there's grass everywhere, we have some cows, we've started bee-keeping, we have another well. Oh, and we built the fishpond, and it leaks and drains out every night, so we've had it mended and lined and think it will be all right now. We had a mongoose to keep down the snakes but it bit me – and died. And I had to have an anti-rabies injection and became allergic and swelled up unrecognisably. Now, forget about Rikki Tikki Tavi, I don't go near the mongoose we've got.'

She still has little or no private life, the flat was full of neat piles of letters, waiting to be answered, she was off back to Bangladesh in the morning so she knew it would mean a two or three in the morning finish, if she was to deal with them this time around. When she's back in this country she is virtually besieged with invitations and requests. She's relaxed and happy.

'The film didn't make me tense, I was only worried that I could do well enough for the orphanage, it's a responsibility when you realise that the whole success of the project might depend on whether people really like you or not. But, in a way, the film was kind to me. It doesn't show me being boring, reading books, daydreaming, all of which I do. But once I'd found out that it didn't matter to you that I wasn't religious, that I did have faults – and a temper – then I was able to be relaxed. The first two films were so hugely successful that I was frightened that we wouldn't do so well with the third, but it was all right.

'And now the only thing – the only thing, ha – is to raise the money to keep the place going. It costs £10 000 a month and some months we get very low and I start to think, God, how are we going to feed them? – and somehow we manage.'

And she flew back – to the orphanage and the children, who still call her Pat Mummy.

CHAPTER NINE

LIVING WITH AIDS

Richard Rector started as our guide to a documentary none of us wanted to make but all of us knew we had to. And Richard became more than a guide – he became the subject, even the hero, of the story that we discovered in the end we wanted the whole world to hear.

Richard will, still, be seen by many as a brave man serving a cause. Others will regard him as a twentieth-century leper, deserving to be exiled from the rest of us. Richard is dying of AIDS. His time is running out. But he's become a man with a mission, a man determined to eliminate ignorance, to confront prejudice – and to encourage compassion in the rest of us. The rest of us, that is, who will live on after Richard, and who must learn how to fight this frightening and lethal, epidemic. So this young man, facing the end, wished to show us a beginning.

Richard, a professional educator, was a young Gay man, living in San Francisco. I had asked Jan to go there to find out if there was one person, one person's story, that could illustrate what I felt very strongly all of us needed to know about AIDS: the truth about AIDS. It was clear to me, that in Britain, there was much disinformation, much prejudice and stupidity. At the same time there was no doubting that this was a lethal disease; it was spreading; it affected, to a greater or lesser degree, all segments of society; research looked many years away from discovering an effective treatment, let alone a vaccine. In this country we were being treated to the Ad-man's message of caution, a huge slate gravestone in a quarry, crashing down and – in my view – burying the real message with ambiguous slogans and doomy music. I had been urged, by among others the Terence Higgins Trust, to use *The Visit* to bring home some simple truths. Anything, any truth, was likely to be better than the advertising and the exaggerations of prejudiced moralists crying that the end of the world was nigh.

We chose San Francisco because, there, they were clearly some years ahead of us in coming to terms with the realities of AIDS. The Golden City had long been a Mecca for homosexuals, at one time they flaunted their difference and their minority power, now they were being decimated by what their detractors wanted to label as a 'gay disease'. But AIDS can, and does, affect all groups. And the Gay community of San Francisco was winning the admiration of the world for the way it sensibly tackled the epidemic, and wanted the rest of the world to benefit from its experience. Richard was working with a local authority, lecturing, researching, advising worried people from all over the world. He worked frenetically hard – he didn't have much time. Nobody at that time could say exactly how long, that never seemed possible, but certainly nobody knew of anybody with full-blown AIDS lasting longer than six or seven years. And Richard had been fully infected for five years. In Britain, life expectancy after the onset of full-blown AIDS is fractionally over nine months ... Richard talked to Jan about what kind of person we might want to film: heterosexual, homosexual, married, single, a drug user victim, a victim who was the result of blood transfusion? Man, woman or child? As he discussed it with her, it became obvious that we had what we needed – in Richard. She telephoned home. Alex and I agreed immediately. Jan had joined forces with Barbra Paskin, a researcher and producer who lives in Hollywood and with whom I had worked many times over the years. She has always been the key person in much of the location work achieved by Barry Norman's weekly *Film 90* (or whatever year) programme. Her talent for getting on with people was an essential help to Jan, besieged by scores of organisations, dozens of people to see and check facts with. We told them both to set up the filming and made preparations to fly to San Francisco, always one of my favourite cities.

It was to be the start of ten days that will remain indelibly

Philip with his medal at Buckingham Palace

TOP LEFT: *Philip's momentous first steps*
TOP RIGHT: *Philip walking with Vanessa in the university grounds*
BOTTOM: *Philip at the Dayton Police Academy – with revolver*

TOP: *Pat Kerr surrounded by 'her' children*
BOTTOM: *Pat Kerr and a new baby for the orphanage*

Richard, a man with a cause

TOP: *Richard lecturing school teachers about AIDS*
BOTTOM: *Flowers in the ocean each time a friend dies*

TOP: *Group 'holding' session*
BOTTOM: *Katy, autistic poet and 'holding' achievement*

The first sight of baby David in Scotland

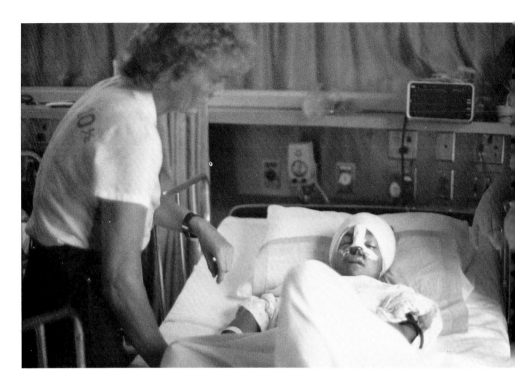

TOP: *In hospital in America after yet another operation, with Marjorie*
BOTTOM: *David and Marjorie today*

etched on my memory. The men and women I met there were among the bravest and the least self-pitying I have ever known. They were never less than generous, understanding and giving with all of us. The agony of their situation wasn't something they talked about in terms of gaining our compassion or pity, only in terms of helping the rest of us understand what it was we were all about to have to face and deal with.

Richard lived with his friend, and lover, Erik von Muller, a handsome young man, dark-haired, athletic and smiling – a wealthy and successful real estate agent. Erik was HIV positive which meant that he had the virus but had not, yet, developed full-blown AIDS. He might go for years, for the rest of his life, without getting AIDS. But, on the other hand, it could happen any day. For him, and Richard, life went on. He was good at selling houses but these days he took along his woman partner, when he was selling to heterosexual customers, because this somehow gave assurance to prospective purchasers. It meant that, implicitly perhaps, Erik was retreating back 'to the closet', to avoid confrontation with those who may have feared that his 'lifestyle' was literally threatening their lives.

Richard had already watched 250 of his friends in the city's Gay community die from AIDS – 250. Each time he had travelled to a small beach, not far from the Golden Gate Bridge, and thrown into the ocean a red rose, sometimes a bunch of roses. He would pause and, silently, say goodbye to yet another friend, yet another victim of this remorseless epidemic. His daily battle, professionally, was somehow to educate the unthinking and unaware population of the United States, to take the 'leper' label away from the victims, remove the stigma that drove so many sufferers to hide their condition, even to die neglected and rejected. Richard's task was also to reach these doomed young men and give them comfort. But how do you comfort 250 people?

'That's a hard one, because you just do it individually. Every person with AIDS, every one that I've been with, has that fear of the stigma. But we are fearful as a general population and this dreadful thing has just moved through our population. So one by one, I try to give them hope. Yes, the hope of surviving, somebody will one day; and the hope of a cure being discovered. It may be years, even decades away but, if you're dying you can truly believe that doctors and researchers might come up with a dramatic cure at the last moment. Remember, this is the country which invented the eleventh-hour ending in all the western films, with the cavalry, bugles blowing, Indians fleeing, charging over the hill at the last moment. And then there is hope – of justice. The hope that we won't be blamed, that my friends who are dying won't have to go to the grave with the added stigma that they infected the world with this epidemic. Society as a whole has coined the term "the Gay Disease", even "the Gay Plague" and now we have to die from the disease and suffer the stigma of knowing that we are blamed for something that threatens everybody. But viruses can't discriminate, they don't know whether you're black, white, male, female, Gay or straight. It has swept through the Gay community because our lifestyle and habits made us more vulnerable. Now we are responding to that, changing our patterns, behaving in a way that won't threaten our lives. But it is just as much a threat to the heterosexual community. It's taking a long time to show up in the same terrifying numbers, but it's there. It's a virus and there are many ways of catching it, many ways for heterosexuals to be infected. And it is lethal – for everybody. And it is growing in size as an epidemic – threatening everybody.

'I have friends who will tell their parents and work colleagues that they have leukaemia, or cancer, for fear of being ostracised from their family at the very time they need them most. When these families find out, they tend to back off and say "wait a minute, you didn't tell me you had AIDS". And if I say to them: "Now, why should the fact that it's AIDS affect the quality of your compassion, the measurement of your caring and loving for that individual?" they will almost always respond: "Well, he didn't tell me he was Gay when he first discovered that, so it's part of his world, and he didn't want to share it with me, except now he has AIDS and he wants my help".'

I smiled at Richard. The analogy – even the syllogism – was

effective and to the point. But, equally, when you're dealing with fear and blind prejudice, you can't expect everybody's logic systems to be persuaded by adversarial discussion, or philosophical comparison. The Gay community, in San Francisco, has been 'out' in the open for many years now. It is an articulate and well-represented group, balanced enough to admit that much of their flamboyant behaviour is hardly likely to draw sympathy and understanding from a national population with more than its share of 'red-necks' and bigots. It is the same nation that still burns crosses in front of the houses of white liberals, or 'uppity' blacks; consigns Latin Americans, Jews and many European immigrants to the ghettos. The honesty in the Gay community, which admits that it has, until this threat, been a largely promiscuous group, is not well-matched in the larger, heterosexual community. There, it takes more honesty than is usually shown for husbands to admit infidelities, or for wives to confess their own unfaithfulness. That deceit hides much of the spread of the HIV virus among the general population, like the tip of the iceberg, only revealed when the virus – which can be dormant for years – turns into AIDS.

Richard himself is what he calls a 'proud Gay man' and is especially proud of the way the Gay community has come to terms with the epidemic. He is the son of a regular soldier. For him, it was particularly hard to 'come out' and it was years before he told his mother and father, divorced now but still living in the New England town where he was brought up. Then, he had to tell them that not only was he Gay but that he had AIDS. 'I had to give them the double whammy, as we say,' he told me. When he mentioned AIDS to his sister, in a telephone call, saying, 'I have AIDS,' she said, 'Oh, how many?' 'I then had to explain that I didn't have a staff of helpers, or aides, but a disease.'

They, in fact, took the news very well. His mother, who was already a religious person became more so and his father took pride in the honesty of his son's action in declaring himself, under difficult circumstances. Erik's mother now also knows that her son has the HIV virus, could become an AIDS

sufferer. When he broke the news to her, she wept but he told
her: 'I want someone to turn to, someone who will accept me
in my totality, someone I can discuss my problems with,
someone who accepts that I'm Gay, that from time to time
I've had a lover, and I want to be able to talk with my mother
about my love problems as well as anything else. I don't want
to leave that whole portion of my life out of our relationship.'
She responded well, so well that Erik says 'Now, we're good
friends, we're best friends.'

Every night, every spare moment that we weren't filming,
we spent with the two boys. They were, and still are, just
about the nicest pair of young men I have ever met. They were
fun, amusing, intelligent and witty. They made jokes, about
Gays, even about AIDS, that took our breath away. But, then,
it has often been black humour that has kept all of us on
the *Visit* team going. (For instance, on Philip Olds, from a
cameraman: 'If he talks like that once more, then I'm going to
unscrew one of his bloody wheels and chuck it in the river.'
Or: our 'sparks', when filming a sequence in San Quentin, on
death row, 'I'm frightened to ask where the electric plugs are,
unless you promise me it's the Gas Chamber they have here
and not the electric chair.') We, ourselves learned a great deal
about AIDS, a great deal to reassure many of the apprehensions
we might have felt before leaving Britain. It is a vulnerable
virus, quite easy to kill – often simple detergents will do it. It
is nevertheless lethal and its reputation alone has caused
parents to keep children away from school if they think there
is a child with AIDS in the same class. In fact, before we left
Glasgow to film this particular *Visit*, I thought it best to have
a chat with the whole crew and answer what questions I could.
They were reassured that they couldn't catch it from food,
plates, knives and forks, or shaking hands. As they left our
cramped office, in Broadcasting House, I noticed that our
electrician was limping. 'What's up, have you hurt your leg?'
I asked, in sympathy. He looked a little embarrassed and
hesitated quite a while before replying:

'Well, you see, Desi, I didn't know we were going to have
this wee talk. And I see now that there was nothing to be

afraid of. But I didn't want to miss the trip – but even more I didn't want to risk catching AIDS. So –' and he finished the sentence in rush, 'I went to the nursing Sister, here in the BBC medical centre, and, I've had an anti-tetanus injection.' The rest of what he had to say was drowned in roars of laughter from everybody else. As we spluttered and explained that all he had managed to do was give himself a sore behind, and no special protection against AIDS, he grinned and countered: 'Ah well, it'll come in handy if I cut myself.'

But we were not to be left in doubt for long about the real nature of AIDS. Paul Volberding is the man in charge of the AIDS programme at San Francisco General Hospital. He's Richard's friend and personal doctor. He was an oncologist, treating cancer patients, before the AIDS epidemic. He thought he would be used to that most stressful area of medicine, where there is no cure and the emphasis must therefore be on caring instead. But: 'I trained as a cancer specialist and I have to say that nothing in my training led me directly to be able to deal with a disease like this one. It affects people the same age as many of the doctors and nurses taking care of the patients. It's disfiguring, it's stigmatising, it's essentially always lethal. It causes dementia. It is a bad, bad disease, in all possible senses – *and it's transmissible.* So, there are many reactions to it, at all levels and even at our professional level we find it difficult to admit that it could still be spreading, and still be as bad as it appears to be.'

Paul is married, to a doctor who works in the same hospital and they have two children and a new baby, and an enviable Californian lifestyle. But their own life, their marriage, has been threatened by AIDS. Paul's role, leading the fight against AIDS, might have been something for Molly to admire, to bring them closer together. But, instead, it came close to breaking them. He told me: 'The worst moment for us as a couple was during the first year when we were afraid of catching the virus ourselves. We couldn't even talk about it to each other, there was so much fear about.'

And Molly added: 'Rather than being able to comfort him or reassure him, or even just listen to him, I had to say "I can't stand to talk to you about this – you either have to decide to stop doing the work with these patients or to continue and not use me as a buffer." The worst thing for me, you can imagine how I felt telling him that, was thinking about Paul dying, but not just thinking of him dying but thinking of the interval between him getting sick and then dying. I couldn't imagine how I would be able to cope with that and the fear it would create in the rest of us. I wondered whether we would have to say: "Paul, you can't come home any more." '

But Paul went on: 'We, those of us working with these patients were tested. It was the most frightening day of my life, I was so sure that I was going to find that I was infected and I just didn't know what I was going to do about it. And then we got the test result back and it was negative and it changed everything. It told me that anybody can work with these patients. If I wasn't infected, then my staff weren't going to be – and no-one was going to be.' But still the patients were dying – when we were there – at the rate of two a day, in San Francisco alone. In Ward 5A of the San Francisco General Hospital there are only AIDS patients; it's now virtually a wing of the hospital. Norman Fowler visited there when he was Secretary of State for Social Services. Richard may have to be there as a patient; he goes in regularly for tests, he has already had several of the classic AIDS illnesses. It has now been discovered that the virus is in his brain: eventually it will lead to dementia. But in the meantime, he goes to counsel friends, to advise patients and their close ones. He also has to take part in the decision to let a patient die – to turn off the life-support machine. Just before we arrived to film, he had been the one asked actually to perform the action. The patient was a dear friend, wasted and beyond recovery, in pain – in need of death.

Richard told me: 'Through each and every one of my friend's deaths I've lived my own. This time it was very much so. His mother called me and asked me to be there in the morning when they were going to take the decision to uncouple him from the respirator. And I went there and we all made the decision, with the doctor, and they looked at me and the doctor said, "Do you want to have the honour?" – of turning the machine off, that is. So I did. And I stepped back and I looked at Jack lying in the bed and we began to take off the tubes, one by one, and the machine was off and he was breathing very, very slowly. And I sat down and I watched him and finally I went up and touched him and I said, "You know, it's okay, you've fought a hard battle."' Richard choked and paused, a long pause, remembering that scene. 'You know, it's all right, it's good to talk about it.' He went on: 'And I said to Jack, "You can leave now, you really can, it's okay." And at the same time there was a part of me went with him. Maybe it was my own fear of dying, that I was finally able to give up, and not feel guilty for being alive, and know that death doesn't have to be that darkness. Yes, it's unknown but so is AIDS. And I am walking through that, I think with my head held high. And I think I can do the same with death.'

In the Gay community in San Francisco it is not possible to find one person whose life has not been touched, changed, by the death of a close friend or relative. Erik and Richard made a strong, supportive couple – even with the threat of the future almost too unbearable to contemplate. But Erik's previous partner, dearly loved for the ten years of their relationship, died of AIDS. With Frank, Erik had already seen what may lie ahead with Richard. He told me: 'The first time Frank was hospitalised, I had asked the doctor: "Is he going to die?" and he had said "Yes" and I had said, "What's going to happen to me?" And he said, "I don't know, make a will." And on about the eighth day I was in the room with him and I felt him starting to die and I started to scream and yell at him and I said, "Don't you dare do this to me, I'm not ready, don't you dare do this."

'And he opened his eyes and he smiled and he said, "All right" – and he went home about eight days after that and on the way out about five different people came up and congratulated him and said, "We never expected you to leave here." And that happened one more time, in February, and he had pneumonia and his temperature was 107 or 108 and they couldn't get it down and we had the windows open to the cold San Francisco air and he developed a resistance to the drug to treat pneumonia and then he had pneumosistis and they were ready to throw their hands in again. And once again I saw death overcome him and it was a physical change, a tangible thing. And this time I was more quiet and I said: "Frank, I know it's a lot to ask, but I'm still not ready." And he opened his eyes and pulled through one more time with immense courage, because as it turned out what he had to face was not pleasant. That was in February and by September the pain was so bad that we were discussing his suicide. I had given him a trip to Hawaii for Christmas and we decided to go through with it. But by then he weighed about 100 pounds and he'd lost control of his legs so he had to travel there by wheelchair – and he never left the chair, he sat and watched the sea and the sand.... And when we came back he lost control of his bowels. And he looked at me and he said "No" and I understood. And we had a volunteer from the hospice organisation come in to the house and help me nurse him. And after three days Tom, the volunteer, called me into the room. Frank had been in coma for three days. So I went into the bedroom and Tom left and I held Frank. And he opened his eyes and he died. That was remarkable, it was a gift to me. Frank went a long way when he died but he left me a lot, he made me a larger person and it took me a long time to take that experience and learn to live with it.'

'But,' I asked. 'Having lived through that searing, personal experience, do you not find it almost unbearable to think that you may have to go through it again – with Richard?'

'In a sense yes, but death has become an organic part of my life and we can't hide it – or hide from it. If Richard becomes ill, if he dies in my arms, then that's, that's what happens.' His voice stuttered slightly, strengthened and went on, 'I can't run away from it and I wouldn't exchange the closeness, the friendship, that Richard has brought to my life and I wouldn't give that away for the hope that I would never have to face something so difficult again. It's trite to say that I could be run over by a bus, it's very trite to say it in front of someone who has a disease as devastating and vicious as AIDS. But it is important to keep an understanding of our own mortality, and the fact that we are all going to die – and not let it overcome us. I love Richard. It's worth it.' Those last three words were delivered slowly, individually and with pain.

The camera stopped. I looked round the room. John McNeill, our cameraman, was wiping his eyes, as was Brian Milliken, the recordist, everybody misted over with truth and hurt. I found I had been leaning forward, holding my hand on top of Erik's. 'Are you sure?' I asked. Erik knew immediately what I meant. 'Yes, I want it known. It may help someone else – there are so many thousands who have yet to face all this. It may help a little.'

Richard lectured schools, teachers, business groups. Richard visited people newly struck by AIDS, set up help lines, counselled relatives, helped them put the affairs of the dying in order, come to terms with the dying itself. His work, his example helped to counter the zealous fervour of single-minded, so-called men of God, like the Reverend Louis Sheldon, who runs an anti-AIDS lobby from the state capital, Sacramento. He reminded me of other militant and opinionated clerics at home, like Ian Paisley: unswerving in their belief that their way is the only way of God – and they are the only guides. Rev. Sheldon calls his organisation The Coalition for Traditional Values, and it is basically a vehement anti-Gay lobby. Questioned about heterosexual sufferers, he claims that sometimes a man cannot resist his urges, then he must be pitied and forgiven: but not Gays. 'God made Adam and Eve – not Adam and Steve,' he intoned on the steps of the Capitol, this cliché pun being the slogan that most usually arouses his prejudiced congregations.

At the Anglican cathedral in San Francisco, they welcome and comfort AIDS sufferers, and Alan Jones, the Deacon, a Welshman, far from his valleys and in the middle of another country's epidemic, believes that AIDS demands a Christian response and mustn't be seen as divine retribution for licentiousness, or the wrath of God, wreaked upon the promiscuous. But he does understand how such mediaeval beliefs can spread. 'The trouble is that illness is a great metaphor as well as an actual fact and it's something that is often tied in with the notion of punishment. So, when you throw illness and punishment and sex together, it's very explosive and people become frightened and they want someone to punish, to call to account. There is still too much fear and ignorance in even the most modern of our societies. In fact I think AIDS has done many of us a great deal of good. It is a tremendous opportunity for the Church to understand what its own vocation is and to regard that aspect of the world, that I choose to call the infinite preciousness of human beings – regardless of who they are, or what they've done.'

Richard told me they call the long-term survivors Generals; he took me to meet Bobby his friend, one of the original Generals, one of the first two dozen people in San Francisco to be diagnosed. Bobby had been in hospital half a dozen times with skin cancer, lung infections, and many other opportunistic infections that invade an AIDS patient. They'd sent him home, with his hospice helper, to see him to the end. Afterwards Richard told me: 'When I was first diagnosed I was the baby, only just starting. They had gone for several years – now I'm a General myself, almost the longest surviving. And that's bad. While the others were there it meant there was more hope of surviving. Now I'm in the firing line.' Six weeks after we filmed the scene with Bobby, he was dead. He was thirty-nine (he looked more than sixty). He was the 1904th person to die of AIDS in San Francisco. Richard has his own counsellor, Ruby Trauner, from the organisation called Shanti, who helps him come to terms with what is ahead. He cares mostly that when it happens it shouldn't drag on, distressing Erik, hurting his friends. He says he will always have enough pain-killers handy to take care of the problem.... It is not a city, nor a time, nor was this the person, to discuss the ethics or otherwise of euthanasia, or suicide. The more all of us knew Richard, the more we ourselves ached at the inescapable path ahead of this gentle man, who was guiding us. When we should have been helping him....

Elizabeth Taylor was speaking, wonderfully, for the AIDS sufferers, fund-raising for the care needed, the research that had to take place. President Reagan finally committed national resources to the research programme and the overstretched medical teams. But Richard, for all of us, said it more effectively, more poignantly than I could ever have believed.

The film was an extended edition of *The Visit*, 75 minutes long instead of the normal 50. It produced a considerable stir when it broadcast. Richard and Erik flew to Britain for the launch of the series; they both appeared on *Wogan*. Letters, the right kind of letters, began to flow in. Richard who had already been lecturing in the States, coast to coast, was asked to station himself in Europe (first Norway, then Denmark) and work for the International Red Cross, setting up advice centres, counselling services, preparing the rest of us for what he knew from experience was ahead of us.

And three years later the most important news to pass on is the fact that Richard is still alive. He's working in Copenhagen. He and Erik have split up, completely amicably, because, at best, they were only seeing each other once a year. Their loyalty and friendship for each other still remains, their concern also. Richard has now had AIDS for more than six years.

And Richard is married. Astonishing? – yes, we all thought so. But, then, perhaps not. He met and married Kirsten Nansen, a Danish social worker whom he had known for two years. They have been working together on international AIDS projects. Richard has been lecturing, advising on four continents and in forty countries. He has, at times, been very ill. His weight is down, he looks thinner (it barely seems possible that he could), but the eyes still twinkle and the energy, the charm, and the persuasion for his cause are still first in evidence. He's been planning projects for the AIDS decimated villages of Uganda and other countries in Africa. He's been made a 'Global Commissioner' for the World Health Organisation (WHO). It isn't just that he's still alive – that is remarkable – it's that he is still so energetically right in the middle of the campaign to speed research into a vaccine, to prepare countries (who may still think it's mostly a Gay disease, or drug-related) for the dreadful increases that he and WHO feel sure will spread (on a deceptively slow curve at the beginning) into heterosexual communities around the world.

The WHO commission on AIDS helps set up policies and reviews, and produces global strategies. They know that in places like Africa and South America the disease is devastating the heterosexual population. They fear that, in this country, in Europe and the USA, we may believe that, because the first predictions have not yet happened, there is far less to worry about among the heterosexual population. The indication, from the overall figures of all sexually transmitted diseases, that young people have shown no substantial change in lifestyle, or reduction in the number of sexual partners in their lives may mean that the 'incubation' of the epidemic is going on at present, and the full scale onslaught has yet to happen. It almost certainly doesn't mean that we can regard AIDS as something we needn't fear, won't touch us, and can therefore put to one side. WHO aren't trying to spread panic – they do want concern and awareness. Their estimates for the spread of HIV in the years to come can hardly leave anybody feeling complacent. At present, as the International AIDS conference in San Francisco was told in the spring of 1990, there are estimated to be 6-8 million people who are HIV-infected, in the world. Seven hundred thousand of them have full-blown AIDS. *But* by the year 2000, WHO believe that, on the present reading of the figures, there will be between 15 and 20 million people in the world who will be HIV-infected – and 75 per cent of them will be through heterosexual transmission. The other, literally morbid statistical forecast is that the rate at which heterosexuals become infected is doubling every year; people who are HIV positive will, on average, develop AIDS within ten years – and the average life span left to a person, once AIDS has been diagnosed, is 9.2 months. It makes Richard more of a miracle, as a survivor, than ever.

So, why did this 'proud Gay man' marry, and what kind of marriage is it? – as ever he has been refreshingly frank and disarmingly amusing about it. He and Kirsten met when both were devastated by the deaths of many close friends, from AIDS. They had been discussing the values, the vital importance, of relationships – and how, somehow, they are often not 'validated' when you die, leaving an individual in a continuing series of devastating and emotionally tearing departures, with no substantial evidence that all this love and friendship was effective, or even there at all. 'So that's it,' he said. 'It was a case of "let's validate our relationship", the validation is very, very important – it may only be a piece of paper but it's a piece of paper that really means something to us. It confirms our relationship to each other, it makes legal our friendship and love and sharing.'

Richard has told his parents and they were delighted. He explained that there wouldn't be any grandchildren from him for them – and he explained to us that it was for the obvious reason of not creating an AIDS baby: he didn't have any problem with sex, he joked.

He has no regrets about the film, indeed he uses it as teaching material; he has no regrets about what he discovered about himself by talking to us – 'It was astonishing, I thought I had been through all the self-analysis it was possible to undertake. But, somehow, making the documentary crystallised a great deal for me and Erik. The hardest part was missing all of you, when you finished filming. It was wonderful coming over to London when the film was broadcast and seeing you again. It was even more wonderful seeing that you had made such a fair and sensitive job of editing it together – it was almost too painful seeing, again, our good friends who had died since the filming, but it confirmed our feeling that we could humanise this epidemic, make people aware of the fact that we all must face it together; we all need each other, we all need all the compassion that we can give each other.

'But it was fun making the film, we had fun with all of you, we shared the same terrible jokes.'

Richard is as well as can be expected, worried whenever his work takes him to the Far East or Africa, and he is too far away from Western medicine to feel entirely comfortable. But, while he never makes light of the situation as a whole, he always plays down his own position, his own future. He refuses to devote time to worrying about that. But those of us who hugged him, with almost desperate intensity, last time we saw him, we worry. In helpless, admiring affection, we worry. But that is what we learned from the film, and what I hope the viewers have now learned also. . . .

Erik is still well, happy and selling houses in San Francisco. He feels happy for Richard – a little surprised – but delighted that both of them are still able to count themselves as strong for their friends, and not in need of strength because of their own extremis. He enjoyed the film, still does in retrospect. He also says he learned from it. He told Jan: 'I think it has done an immense amount of good, as a film. I think Desmond was looking for a hero, because he understood that if he found one – not created one but discovered one – then the viewers would be drawn into a better and more sensitive understanding of what this is all about. He was right to do this. But it's made me understand that there is a hero in all of us. I think it is in every human's make up and I think it has to be balanced by the negative side in all of us. The quality of the hero, balanced against the depth of the shadow. That, I believe came out in the documentary.

'I think he was looking for a hero to present to the British public, to open the can so to speak, so that his hero could help the people who will have to be the heroes in your country. And you are going to need your heroes.'

CHAPTER TEN

RESCUE FROM AUTISM: THE STORY – AND THE ROW

We receive many letters from parents in pain – they want us to investigate a new treatment, a 'miracle' cure even; but they really want us to share the dilemma of not knowing where to turn to save their children. It isn't possible to follow all the paths they point at, all the hopes they clutch at. It is impossible not to be moved by their desperate need to do something, almost anything, rather than accept a diagnosis that is bleak, chilling – and hopeless. Such is the case with autism. We have, ever since we started *The Visit*, received almost unbearable pleas from parents, at their wit's end with helplessness and exhaustion, wanting some way out for the autistic child.

Then we were asked to look at the work of a remarkable American child psychiatrist, Dr Martha Welch, who had spent fifteen years developing a form of therapy for the autistic child, called 'Holding'. It was dramatic, intense, almost violent – but for many parents and their children it worked. Nobody claimed that it was a miracle cure, nobody used that word, but they did claim that if 'cure' meant taking your place in a normal school, in the right class for your age, going on to a job, relating with the world – and being happy – then this treatment did that in a great many cases. It was being practised, here in Britain, by several dedicated therapists who had become disciples of the system and Martha Welch. Children, who had always been withdrawn from the world, from their families, from love, were emerging through 'Holding Time': children who had been consigned, by diagnosis, to a future that for most parents is too painful to consider. Take one phrase from one of the pamphlets that were sent out by this country's National Autistic Society, when parents first contacted them, distressed by the discovery that their child was autistic: 'The handicap of autism is devastating ... no-one knows what causes autism ... there is as yet no cure, it is a lifelong handicap.' It was unsurprising, to me at least, that such parents should feel that the one element in care, in love, that keeps all of us going in these circumstances, was missing – they need, really need, the right to hope.

We went to Connecticut, to a suburb of Greenwich, looking almost a postcard of the American Dream, New England style. There in a white frame-house Martha Welch runs what she calls her 'Mothering Centre'. There we found parents who, in some cases, had travelled for days with their autistic children, willing to try almost anything, hoping to find that this treatment was the answer to their prayers and hopes. The scene in her study, the floor layered with huge cushions, was like a Hogarth drawing of bedlam. Mothers clutching their children, tight, forcing them to meet their eyes (few autistic children will make eye contact, most hate any physical contact), screaming at them: 'Look at me, look at me'. Adults crying, mothers weeping, husbands clutching wife and child, sobbing too. The tensions were unbearable. In the middle of it all a young immaculately dressed and groomed American blonde, make up and jewellery in place, eyes alert, body poised – Martha Welch, conducting this giant discordant human orchestra of misery and passion, with skill, with precision, with success.

And her successes were remarkable, we filmed any number of them. Her theory, endorsed by the eminent behavioural psychologist and Nobel laureate, Professor Nikolaas Tinbergen, and worked into shape by her during fifteen years of careful research and practice, was that by forcefully holding the autistic child, by forcing the parental bond back on the child, even against their struggling resistance, you could re-establish the connection between mother and child, the broken bond could be healed. It stemmed from her studies which seemed to show that an early traumatic experience (even in the very earliest infancy) would cause a breaking of the mother-child bond and frequently result in autism. The possibility that much of autism is caused by brain damage is still the most commonly regarded, but not yet proved, theory among establishment experts in the field. We met youngsters who had been totally withdrawn – and were now to all intents and purposes normal. We met parents who had struggled for years with other treatments – and not achieved any kind of breakthrough, until they had tried Holding.

Martha, invariably looking more like a top model or a power-dressing, advertising agency executive, is herself the mother of a bright ten-year-old boy, Bramwell. She and her doctor husband divorced some years ago. She is the author of *Holding Time* (published in the UK by Century-Hutchinson), a book about Holding with one of the longest sub-titles ever: *How to eliminate conflict, temper tantrums, and sibling rivalry and raise happy, loving, successful children*. It is, as she calls it, a resource book for parents. It offers holding as a technique for dealing with a range of children's disturbances – she uses it on her own son, who frequently feels the natural resentment of a child with a single working parent, whose work keeps her away from him and answering his needs. She even, rather refreshingly, quotes him in the book as an endorsement of the practice.

'After holding you feel as though you have never been angry and never will be.'

The method of holding is difficult and exhausting for both child and parent. What's more Martha believes very strongly that no amount of holding with an autistic child can fully succeed if the father is not also part of the treatment. With divorced and separated parents this sometimes spells out a difficult-to-accept future. After what can be hours of struggle, 'the rejection', there is then a period of calm, of sobbing acceptance, 'the resolution'. By building these sessions parents have been able to make contact with children who previously had done no more than sit in corners, flapping their hands, dribbling, refusing to speak, to look at any person, withdrawn completely from our world into a world of their own. And Holding has come to this country. One of its practitioners, Jasmine Bayley, a schoolteacher who was drawn, as a home tutor of disturbed children, into caring for autistic children, now runs an English Mothering Centre from her home in Teddington; there are others in the West country and in the North. She travelled, while we were filming, to see Martha and discuss the next step she might take to expand the work – 'My little mothering nests,' Martha called it all. Through her we met, when we returned to Britain, Michael Selwyn aged three – and autistic.

When Michael was first born he seemed perfect. It took nearly two years of observation and worrying to reach the diagnosis that Michael is autistic. The problem seemed to show itself with the arrival of his baby sister, Emma, nearly two years younger than him. Nicky Selwyn gave up breast-feeding Michael in order to nurse the new-born child. She believes that this action, almost an obvious breaking of the bond, triggered or caused the autistic withdrawal of her son. She and her husband David went to the National Autistic Society for help, they received a quantity of literature. 'I found a lot of it very, very distressing because it all seemed to be saying there is no hope, there is no future, these children are not curable, they will waste away in institutions. They are ineducable. Now I know that many if not most autistic children do wind up in institutions, but I don't feel that anybody has the right to take away a parent's hope. I felt I wanted encouragement, not depressing, I wanted to pioneer, not give up – I wanted to break down barriers and I was distressed that the first people I turned to weren't helpful.'

The National Autistic Society is a knowledgeable body – but knowledgeable bodies can be, and have been, wrong. I remember the protests from the medical establishment over the work being done in the Peto institute in Budapest, called Conductive Education, with severely handicapped children, whom experts had said would never walk, should not be encouraged to think they ever could. They came off the plane walking, having been taken there, against expert advice in this country, by parents who refused to give up hope.

Like that case I felt that it was proper for us, as a documentary team, to look at Holding, if it gave parents hope, which it quite clearly did. It was not for us to judge or particularly to proselytise. We asked the National Autistic Society if they would take part in the programme, express the reservations they had and suggest how to qualify the views of parents, who refused to see Holding as anything other than a cure – and held their own children up as an example. They suggested instead that we should not be making the programme at all; it would give false hope to too many people, Holding was not yet proven and the causes of autism were, whatever they were, not solely or even mostly due to the broken maternal bond. We drew breath and persisted. We would still like them to take part, we needed to hear their reservations but it was not improper of us to film the personal reactions of people who *did* believe it was a breakthrough – and for many the answer. Jan went to meet Lorna Wing, a Vice-President of the Society, a distinguished psychiatrist and herself the mother of an autistic daughter, who was put into an institution in her teens when there were barely any facilities available for parents of autistic children. That information came from the press officer of the Society by way of letting us understand that Lorna Wing's distinguished record was reinforced by personal experience. But Lorna Wing was adamant that she did not agree with Holding as a treatment for autism. She didn't think Holding a bad thing, indeed she told me when we filmed an interview with her that she often gave her own daughter many hugs and cuddles. But she thought that it was wrong to think that Holding could be anything even like a cure, might even be disturbing and bad for the parents and the children, if it went 'wrong'. She had written a paper setting herself firmly against it. She had not actually witnessed it but had viewed an unedited home video, shot in Jasmine Bayley's home. She was less than admiring of the fact that Jasmine kept no written records, conducted no parallel research. 'I would say that in my view there is absolutely no evidence to date of its [Holding] effectiveness and looking at it as a possible way of help-ing autistic children it seems inherently unlikely that it will succeed.'

We interviewed Lorna Wing for more than thirty minutes, we were with her for about two hours, but she firmly and politely refused to give even the smallest nod of approval in the direction of this new treatment. We packed up our film gear and left the Willesden headquarters of the Society.

In the meantime Nicky Selwyn and young Michael were doing amazingly well with Holding. We went straight to the Teddington centre to film them and had only just started running the camera when, in the middle of a stress-filled and exhausting 'hold', we heard what had never happened before. Michael spoke. After three years of silence, the tears running down his face, his eyes fixed on his mother's, he said: 'Mama. Mama.'

Nicky told me later, 'I know that there are parents who've tried Holding and don't think it works, there are others who have reservations about the violent and naked kind of emotional confrontations that it produces between mother and child. But I'm just so grateful for having discovered it. I was given hope when I didn't have any hope. And already I'm seeing changes, I've got something to work towards. I was in a situation where there was nothing to lose and now there is so much I can do.'

Martha Welch flew to London, with Bram who accompanies her nearly everywhere (one of the more interesting chapters in her book is how to deal with the stress caused in children who have working mothers) to visit her 'nests'. In the garden of Jasmine Bayley's home, flower-filled, humming with bees, she explained to me why she thinks it has taken her so many years even to begin to gain acceptance for her theories and her treatment:

'In any scientific field – but especially in the area of autism – people are very afraid to accept something that isn't well substantiated over time. But now we're beginning to have that substantiation. As this body of information builds, it's harder and harder not to accept. But you can't blame the professionals, because there have been so many promises about cures for autism and everybody's gotten their hopes up – and then they've been dashed. So everybody nowadays has a wait-and-see attitude. But in my country this attitude is changing from, "Does this work?" to "Why does this work?" and that's the real breakthrough. It's a great step forward.'

'Rescue From Autism' was two films, one based in America, the other in this country. After their transmission we had hundreds of letters from parents praising the work of Martha Welch, some wanting help for their own children but mostly just stimulated into praise by the films. A little later the other letters started coming in. Protests from local Autistic Societies, piles of letters from members. These letters had a disturbing and uncomfortable feel to them. They used many of the same phrases, indeed many of them were absolutely identical in paragraph after paragraph. They all said we were proselytising a cure, behaving evangellically for Martha Welch. They complained that they knew the interview with Lorna Wing had been unfairly edited (it ran twelve minutes, longer than any other interview in the two films or any other interview in other *Visit* programmes). It seemed obvious to me that we were on the receiving end of a lobby, which seemed orchestrated to a degree. In the American Senate, lobbyists often calculate that the effectiveness of any pressure sent to a Senator by mail, is measured by weight. I began to think the same thing was happening to us. It seemed unfair because we were being accused of something we knew we hadn't done – using television to 'sell' the work of somebody in this area and claim it as a cure. We answered all the letters (little Aileen Campbell began to droop over the typewriter by the end of several days) as gently as we could. We were more pleased to hear that more than fifty mothers had contacted Jasmine Bayley to bring their children to her, thus underlining the value of her Mothering Centre.

And then we really were complained about, to the Broadcasting Complaints Commission. The National Autistic Society complained to this independent body that the two programmes gave an unbalanced and unfair picture. There were other similar complaints from local autistic organisations but, sensibly in my view, the Broadcasting Complaints Commission decided to deal with the National Autistic Society's complaint as representative of the other complaints also. As it was our firm belief that the complaints were both inspired and orchestrated centrally, it was, we considered, the only fair way. We had by then been told, through Jasmine Bayley, and several very distinguished psychiatrists who had advised us throughout the making of the documentaries, that at some regular meetings and during the course of one or two speeches, members of these various societies were being urged to add their weight to the complaint and, indeed, were having exact phrases 'suggested' to them.

The next few weeks became a nightmare for our tiny team. The Commission needed to view the programmes on video, several videos. That was simple. Then they needed transcripts of the programmes so as to be able to examine in detail (perhaps even debate meaning at length) every word, every implication of the interviews and the narration. This struck me as an understandable need but still slightly unfair to the programme team, as the words broadcast are heard and not recalled for dissection in this way for the viewers. Then we had to make lengthy submissions answering the many points (more than fifty single items were complained about, some of them frankly rather silly, but still needing response) raised in the many pages of complaint. There were accusations from one of our interviewees, in the United States that we had somehow contrived to invent words and put them on film in her name. This was not only a silly and professionally damaging lie, but easy to disprove. All negative film is retained, it is numbered along the edge, any false editing can be spotted instantly. But all this took hours of time, cost a great deal of BBC money (having the negative made available for inspection, writing for hours on end, lengthy explanations of who said what to whom and why, looking up travel forms and diaries, checking with transcripts, photocopying, posting, sending by courier motor cycle). In BBC Scotland I was still expected to be making the next series of *The Visit* so all this had to be squeezed in. The Secretary of BBC Scotland, James Boyle, was very supportive and friendly, but nevertheless the preparation of a 'defence' was on our shoulders and certainly began to make us all feel rather like the 'accused'. My programme bosses in Scotland were kept aware of all that was going on (I

142

was, under BBC rules, always obliged to copy such correspondence either to them or through them to the person
addressed). I had explained that we had a complete answer,
that the complaint was wrong and could be totally refuted.
Jim Hunter is a veteran of many BBC battles with outside
organisations (his special delight was the in-fighting that
always went on with the Scottish Football Association.) It
must have been that battleground experience that made him
stand his distance from this struggle. He took the view that it
wasn't really his fight – and he may congratulate the winner;
and that had better be me. 'Or else,' is always understood in
these cases. I clearly understood and was grateful that he
didn't – as some bosses are prone to – leap immediately to the
conclusion that because there was a complaint then I and my
team just had to be in the wrong.

But the man who kept all of us sane during the many weeks
that this gritty and depressing experience took was the most
charming, and wise diplomat ever to escape being made British
Ambassador to one of the capital cities of the world, Towyn
Mason, a clever and quick-thinking Welshman, and the Deputy
Secretary of the BBC. Among his many and difficult duties is
the task of dealing with the outside world, when it complains
at the highest level. He has, therefore, become an expert in
understanding the nature of the Broadcasting Complaints
Commission, in discerning what they needed (and what would
just snow them under with unnecessary paperwork and
protest). He had become, like a good doctor, the man to soothe
our frazzled nerves and the burning sense of injustice that one
always feels when wrongly accused. But, most of all, he was
the man who took my immensely long and detailed memos
and distilled them into an acceptable length, still several pages
at a time, and polished the language, immaculately. We dealt
with the accusation that we had interviewed Lorna Wing for
two to three hours and then only used a few minutes. It wasn't
true. We dealt with the suggestion that we were 'selling' a cure
and holding out unreal hope to parents. We produced scores
of letters from people who had written, not in complaint
but in praise. We showed that articles in quality newspapers

describing Martha Welch and Holding had used precisely the same language, similar cases – and not a single complaint, we verified, had come in to the newspapers concerned. This last is surely a classic demonstration that the emotive nature of television causes more people to respond than the same kind of material, in print. Jan produced all her research notes, I sent my commentaries in for analysis. Alex was at pains to show what had been left out in editing and to prove that the reduction in length had been fair and not a distortion.

Again and again we made the point that the *Visit* style was to follow one person or a family, not to do a *Panorama* in comprehensive and complete terms, and that, on many occasions, organisations and the Establishment had tried to stop us making films (as the National Autistic Society attempted to do), but in fact the events we had filmed in the past had led to the creation of charities and to an acceptance of new systems and ideas. We thought this to our credit, rather than otherwise.

Then, a date was set; all three us were required to attend a large dignified building in the lee of Victoria Station in London, together with the 'other side'. Wearing our best suits, and our shoes polished for the day, we turned up, carrying bundles of documents. So did a number of people from the National Autistic Society. But *not* Lorna Wing. Her absence was never explained to us and the thought that she now didn't wish to be associated with the complaint or that there had been disagreement behind the scenes, would be only speculation on our part – but it is the sort of thought that crosses one's mind at tense times like this. The others had already said their say when we were called. They were allowed to stay while we said ours, or rather answered questions from the members of the Commission and from the National Autistic Society. By this time I was so tense I would have confessed to stealing the Crown Jewels. Fortunately the Commission members are wise and careful, and clearly understand this. What is more, they understand television programme-making, with two distinguished broadcasters, such as David Holmes and Peter Hardiman Scott, among them, they were equipped to judge very fairly indeed. Both these men had served in the highest BBC positions, working in Parliament and were veterans of many disputes between, for instance, government and broadcasters, distinguishing themselves for their professional objectivity.

After two hours, it was over. We left – and like GCSES or 'A' levels we knew we had to wait for the result. When it came it was accompanied by a small note from the estimable Towyn Mason – and his secretary had added, at the bottom 'Congratulations'. We went out to dinner, we drank to the future of *The Visit*. I was saddened that we had upset the Society and Lorna Wing, we didn't mean to. Being proved right was no justification for being cocky. But it did confirm that the kind of programme we feel we are best at making is doing the right job for the viewers – even if we sometimes have to stand up and prove that we are right. It is, I feel, important for readers – and viewers – to know that we don't take our responsibilities lightly and that we are 'brought to book' when viewers complain. Usually, I am told, there is some reservation in the findings of the Commission, quite often condemnation. The broadcaster is obliged to publish and broadcast the short form of the adjudication. I'm glad in our case that it did us no harm, indeed, only good. And I can hardly ever forget the parents who said: 'We must be allowed to have hope.' And so endorsed the Commission:

'THE VISIT'
Complaint from the National Autistic Society
Summary of adjudication

The Broadcasting Complaints Commission, who are concerned with fairness and privacy, have adjudicated upon a complaint about two programmes entitled 'Rescue From Autism' in the series, *The Visit*, broadcast on BBC 1 on 9 and 16 November 1988. These programmes dealt with 'holding therapy' as a treatment of autistic children administered by parents. The National Autistic Society and several local societies for people with autism complained that the programmes gave an unbalanced and unfair picture of autism and 'holding therapy'. The Society also complained that their work was dismissed as offering no hope or support.

The Commission consider that a vice-president of the National Autistic Society was given an adequate opportunity in one of the programmes to express her views and those of the Society, and to answer criticisms. The programmes were not unfair to the Society.

The Commission note that the programmes did not set out to compare or show other treatments for autism nor did they assert that 'holding therapy' was a cure, or that nothing else was being done. Although the Commission can understand that some parents of autistic children would find the programmes distressing or even unbalanced, the Commission do not conclude that they were unfair.

20 June 1989

But it may be interesting and helpful (you may want to complain one day!) to see the fair-minded and scrupulous way the Broadcasting Complaints Commission goes about its investigation and findings, by reading the full adjudication:

Complaint from the National Autistic Society
Adjudication

Introduction

On 9 and 16 November 1988, BBC 1 broadcast two programmes entitled 'Rescue From Autism' in the series *The Visit*. These programmes were about the use of 'holding therapy' as a treatment for autism. Advocates of this therapy believe that by 'holding' autistic children, if necessary by force, parents could help or even cure them. The programmes showed the use of 'holding' in both the USA, where it was first developed, and in the UK. The merits of 'holding' were discussed with parents of autistic children, with Dr Martha Welch, who had pioneered and promoted the use of the therapy in the USA, and with Dr Lorna Wing of the National Autistic Society in Britain. Dr Wing expressed the Society's view that 'holding therapy' was not a proven cure for autism and that research was unlikely to find otherwise. The Broadcasting Complaints Commission received several broadly similar complaints from local organisations concerned with the care of autistic children and adults, and one from the National Autistic Society, that the programmes were unfair. The Commission decided to entertain the complaint from the National Autistic Society as representative of the concerns of those local organisations who had also complained.

The complaint

The National Autistic Society complained that the programmes gave an unbalanced and unfair picture of autism and 'holding therapy'. In particular, the programmes strongly implied that 'holding therapy' would provide a cure for autism. This claim was not substantiated in the programmes; no definition was given of what constituted a cure and no interviews were conducted with anyone who had been cured by 'holding'. The Society argued that the children shown in the programmes as examples of the successful use of 'holding' were no more capable than children known to the Society who had not received that therapy. The Society disputed the suggestion in the programmes that if an autistic child began to speak, this represented the beginnings of a cure. Many autistic children spoke. The programmes were therefore misleading. The programmes were also unbalanced in that they failed to mention the successes achieved by alternative forms of management, including education in the specialist schools such as those provided by the Society. Furthermore, although it was acknowledged that 'holding therapy' was a controversial treatment, the programme-makers had not spoken to parents who had found 'holding' to be unsuccessful. The programme effectively put forward the view that 'holding therapy' was the only way of achieving improvements in autistic children.

The Society said they were disappointed to see their efforts dismissed in the programmes as those of 'the establishment' which offered no hope or support to parents. They considered that the use of the terms 'institution' and 'institutionalisation' in connection with the special schools, such as those provided by the Society, was emotive and offensive. The Society said they would be mortified to think they had created nothing but a cold-hearted, unresponsive bureaucracy. They contended that, unlike the proponents of 'holding', they did not offer parents the false hope that their autistic child would be cured but the realistic prospect that the child would be helped to overcome his difficulties and live a more independent life. The Society maintained that specialist teaching in appropriate surroundings led to many autistic children achieving dramatic improvements. Some were able to return to mainstream schools; these children were not, however, cured. The Society maintained that the programme-makers had not conducted adequate research. Had they done so, they would have known that virtually every initial approach to the Society was by telephone and that, in addition to a wide range of literature, each parent received a personalised response from the Society which was as appropriate and sensitive to their individual needs and circumstances as possible. Furthermore, the Society endeavoured to put parents in touch with each other. The results of such contact proved very positive. The Society complained that the programmes included only a small section of a longer filmed interview with Dr Lorna Wing. The Society maintained that the selection had been made to show the Society and Dr Lorna Wing in a negative light and that this was unfair to both.

The Society were concerned by reports that the programmes led to many parents being offered well-meaning advice that 'holding' provided a cure for their autistic children. The Society suggested that the parents, who might already feel guilt that their child's handicap was somehow their fault, were, as a result of *The Visit*, also suffering further guilt if they did not accept 'holding therapy' as the answer to their child's condition.

The BBC's response

The BBC explained that the programmes did not purport to provide a comprehensive survey of all that was being done in the research and treatment of autism. *The Visit* was a series which examined the experience, motivation and feelings of the people on whom it focused: in this case, parents who practised 'holding therapy'. The programmes were as much a portrayal of the attitudes and emotions of these parents as they were a study of the treatment itself.

The BBC maintained that, throughout the programmes, the presenter took care to avoid asserting that 'holding therapy' was a cure or that it was appropriate to all sufferers of autism. The word 'treatment' was used rather than 'cure'. The faith which some had in 'holding therapy' was acknowledged but so were the reservations felt both by the medical establishment and by individual parents. The BBC suggested that the theme of the programmes could be summed up in the words of one of the main participants, a parent of an autistic child: 'Everything which is available to help autistic children which I believe may be of some use without doing any harm I feel has got to be worth a try.'

The BBC rejected the claim that the National Autistic Society had been presented in the programmes as a cold-hearted, unresponsive bureaucracy who believed that nothing could be done to help autistic people. Participants in the programmes had found that the Society's literature was discouraging. It was participants who had used words such as 'institution' and 'institutionalisation'. The National Autistic Society were able to answer criticisms in the programmes through the interview with Dr Lorna Wing, of which almost twelve minutes were broadcast. The BBC did not believe that she gave the impression of being cold-hearted; on the contrary, it was clear that, as herself the parent of an autistic child, she was familiar with the attendant problems. They also maintained that she was given ample opportunity to express the Society's views of 'holding therapy' and autism.

Evidence considered by the Commission

The Commission had before them letters of complaint from the National Autistic Society and various regional autistic societies, a statement in answer to the complaint by the BBC, a response to that statement by the National Autistic Society and observations on that response from the BBC. The Commission read the transcripts and viewed the videos of both programmes. A hearing was held which was attended by representatives of the National Autistic Society and of the BBC.

The Commission's findings

The Commission note that the programmes were primarily concerned with a particular therapy used by some as a treatment for autism. *The Visit* approached this subject through the experience of the parents, children and therapists involved. The Commission accept that, despite the title 'Rescue From Autism', it was not the programmes' intention to explore autism in general or to compare 'holding therapy' with other treatments. The Commission can, however, understand that if viewers failed to recognise this they might consider the programmes to be unfair. The Commission recognise that the National Autistic Society hold views about the origin and treatment of autism which contrast markedly with the views of those who favour 'holding therapy'. The Society also hold different views on what is helpful to parents. The Society believe that it is more comforting and helpful for parents to accept that their autistic child has a life-long disability, and to strive for the best possible development within the limitations of that disability. Proponents of 'holding' consider it more helpful and comforting to give parents the hope of a cure. The Commission consider the Society's dissatisfaction with the programmes stemmed from this essential difference in approach. The Commission do not judge which approach is correct, although they note, as did the programmes, that the National Autistic Society share the generally held medical view. The programmes did not assert that 'holding therapy' was a cure for autism. It did show parents who 'have no doubts' and showed Dr Welch, who described some of her successful cases. The presenter, Desmond Wilcox, appeared to share some of the enthusiasm and hope of parents who practised 'holding'. However, having referred to one autistic child as 'cured by holding', he later said of the same child, 'he is doing well at school in spite of his autism'. In her interview, Dr Lorna Wing asserted that what 'cure' meant in the case of autism was 'a very complex subject'. Dr Welch described 'cure' as 'enjoying normal life'. Dr Wing pointed out that some autistic children become functioning adults without being cured of their autism. The Commission do not consider that it was necessary, in fairness to the subject matter, and in the context of the particular programmes, to enter deeply into this 'complex subject'.

The Commission note that criticisms of the National Autistic Society, and in particular of its literature, stemmed from the experience of individual parents who were unhappy with the Society's approach. These criticisms Dr Lorna Wing was able to answer on behalf of the Society. Moreover, in the Commission's view, Dr Wing had ample opportunity to put her general views, and those of the Society, on the treatment of autism, but she chose to restrict herself to her views on 'holding therapy'. She could have used the opportunity of a lengthy interview to point out the kind of educational help and treatment the Society was providing for autistic children. It has not been suggested to the Commission that she did so, even in untransmitted parts of the interview. Had she done so, 'holding therapy' would have been more clearly seen as only one of various approaches to the treatment of autism. The Commission find that the programmes were not unfair to the National Autistic Society or indeed to Dr Lorna Wing.

The Society complained that the programmes gave an unbalanced and unfair picture of autism and 'holding therapy'. The Commission have noted statements, such as those introducing the second programme, that autistic children were 'labelled incurable and facing a lifetime in an institution'. These might have been taken as implying that 'holding therapy' gave the only hope for improvement in an autistic child and that nothing else was being done to help. In the Commission's view, however, this was not the contention of the programmes, which were only concerned with following the experiences of parents who had tried one specific treatment developed in the United States. While the Commission can understand that some parents of autistic children would find the programmes distressing, and even unbalanced, the Commission do not conclude that they were unfair.

24th May 1989

It was signed by the Chairman and members:

Lady Anglesey
David Holmes
Brigid Wells
Henry McKenzie-Johnson

Since the programmes were shown, the National Autistic Society has become much more enlightened – they are amending their literature about autism to read in a less negative manner; their magazine, *Communication*, has published several letters from parents of autistic children using Holding satisfactorily; and they have referred parents seeking information about Holding to Jasmine Bayley of the Tinbergen Trust. In addition, Nottingham University are carrying out a three-year research project for the DHS, comparing four different 'therapies' for autism, one of which is Holding.

CHAPTER ELEVEN

THE BOY DAVID
THE STORY THAT GOES ON

It is the one story, I've told on television, that everybody, quite without exception, wants to hear more of. It has the romantic, dramatic, and plain hard-hitting qualities of the best adventure tales, detective stories – or a long-running television drama series. The story of the child from the Amazonian jungle, rescued, restored, adopted – by the remarkable couple who have saved his life, created his new life, and rightly won the admiration of millions of people around the world. The story of Ian Jackson, the distinguished consultant and plastic surgeon, and his wife Marjorie, already mother to four children when she took on the role of adoptive mother for a waif from Peru, with huge brown eyes – and no centre to his face.

He had, as a baby, been delivered by his father to the care of some teaching and nursing nuns in a jungle mission, deep in the upper Amazonian basin, in Peru. His face had been destroyed, eaten, by a virulent condition that not infrequently attacks young children among the river bank tribes, and may even have been triggered by a mosquito bite. David Lopez, a member of the Campa Indian tribe, had been brought by dug-out canoe to the only people who might be able to help him, by a father who cared enough in a society where it is not uncommon for deformed children to be abandoned to die. And there was nothing the good nuns could do, his condition was beyond their skills, maybe even beyond their knowledge. He was, eventually, taken by the regular supply plane, that flew the perilous journey over the Andes, to the capital, Lima. And there he was handed over to the Hospital del Niños, a run-down, overcrowded place providing some kind of hospital care for the poor and the desperate. Better than the streets where so many of the poor live, and then beg to live. But not much. At del Niños he was virtually abandoned, within the hospital. He was beyond their skills too, so they kept him, unable to speak, a deformed and tragic baby, with great intelligent eyes, in the corner of a fly-blown ward.

The hospital records for David Lopez are still there, the description of the damage to his face. No upper jaw, no upper teeth, no nose, no upper lip, only a lower jaw, a hole – and those eyes. A Swiss charity worker heard that a famous British surgeon was operating in a nearby clinic; he specialised, she knew, in cranio-facial deformities in children, hare lips, cancer damage, accident damage, birth deformities. She 'kidnapped' little David Lopez from the charity hospital and took him to the clinic mentioned on the local television. There she waited outside the operating theatre for the famous Scottish surgeon to emerge. And when he did she gave him David. Ian Jackson remembers the moment well:

'He was sucking a lollipop. ... So, here was this child with a lollipop in his mouth. The only unusual thing was that the stick of the lollipop came out from a hole about half an inch above his eyes, because with having no roof to his mouth he could bring his lower teeth right up to his forehead. And, of course, the lollipop was being sucked against the base of his skull, several millimetres from the under-surface of his brain. He had lost the greater part of his jaw, his upper teeth were missing, he had no teeth, the upper lip was missing and he had no central area to his face.'

And the story began there. Although it was a long time before most of the facts I've just revealed were really known.

Ian Jackson was Consultant at Canniesburn, the Scottish hospital, when all this started. He lived with his family in a respectable suburb of Glasgow, Bearsden. His skill and his reputation were for remarkable successes restoring the brutally damaged and misshapen, the results of accident or disease, or birth, and he had, therefore, often thought about the reaction of society, us that is, to deformity.

He told me: 'I think in a way there's sometimes much more sympathy for people who are crippled as opposed to people who are facially deformed. You know, the blind people always

154

get the sympathy, whereas the deaf people get ridiculed. And, if you look in literature or painting or history, the ugly people and the deformed people have always been seen as objects of amusement – or evil objects and so I think we have these inbuilt prejudices against people who don't look like we do.'

Alex told me about the boy David, during my first few weeks, while we were working out what kind of series we wanted *The Visit* to be. The story had been reported in the Glasgow papers; it turned out to have been dramatically and horrendously mis-reported. The Catholic Archbishop, and the warm-hearted people of Glasgow had already raised money for him, lots of it. In Lima, Ian had examined David and told the charity worker, Martine, that there was nothing he could do there and then, and both the skills he needed, and the time he needed, were only available back home in Glasgow. So, unless they could get him to Glasgow – sorry. Not brutal nor without compassion, just factual and realistic. It took him aback when he heard that the determined Martine had once again 'kidnapped' David, jumped on a plane from Peru to Britain and was bringing him to Glasgow. Marjorie learned the news as Ian set off for hospital, with a cheery 'You'll just have to do the best you can'.

She went to the airport and remembers the scene well: 'Your heart couldn't fail to go out to him. Here was this tiny, frightened little Peruvian boy, very cold, very scared. He had a little woolly Peruvian hat on, which covered all of his face except for his eyes – and the hole in the centre of his face. He was an odd little figure and terribly pathetic.' Ian added: 'He had all the instincts of an animal. If there was food around, he would eat it whether he was hungry or not. He would never leave anything. If there was a scrap left on anybody's plate, he would eat it. He would eat the butter, he would eat the sugar. And he would use his fingers to do that. And if we gave him anything he would take the object and hide it in his room and he wouldn't let anyone go and look at it.'

Ian and Marjorie Jackson took David into their home and their family – and certainly into their hearts. Ian devised a pattern of surgery, an almost unrelenting pattern, that in many instances would be pioneering. He would of course be giving his services free, his surgical team offered to do so also, but there were still National Health charges that would have to be paid – David was an alien, with no official status in this country and no entitlement to free medical resources. That's where the people of Glasgow came in, raising, when the story appeared, thousands of pounds to protect David. The Jacksons were less than impressed by the tabloid papers which took to calling him 'The Jungle Boy' and said that he had been kept in a cage, then abandoned near the Nuns' mission, left for them to find him – or to die. It was to be many long months before the truth about David's father's journey and how he came to be handed to the nuns was known. The Jacksons, not seeking publicity, wanting only to do their best for the waif they'd taken in, had not been interviewed on television, were shocked enough by tabloid lies and sensationalism to be vigorously anti-media. Alex was insistent that they could be persuaded that our purpose was worthwhile.

By this stage of 'The Boy David' story the Jacksons had moved to live in the United States, where Ian had taken up the post of Head of Reconstructive and Plastic Surgery in the internationally famous Mayo Clinic in Rochester, Minnesota. David was still living as part of the family, loved and much cared for by his new brothers and sisters, Linda, Susan, Sarah and Andrew. Ian was still engaged in the continuing tasks of rebuilding the child's face. He took pedicles of flesh from David's groin to make a nose, part of his tongue to make an upper lip, ribs and slivers of bone from his skull to build a jaw. The process was seemingly unending, much of the surgery had never been attempted before. Because newly transplanted flesh is especially vulnerable to cold, David spent the harsh American winters in Spain with the woman who had been his English teacher in Glasgow, Mary Rodriguez, and her husband Robert. It was an odd, commuting existence, for this South American Indian child, who now spoke Spanish, English, with an American accent and used Scottish phrases. He was still, literally, without a country and allowed only to travel and reside in the United States so long as he was undergoing surgery, which was to be, in any event, for many years to come.

I was travelling to Florida with Esther and the children on a holiday before we really buckled down to making that first series of *The Visit*. Alex – he and I had only known each other a month or two at that stage – urged me to ring the Jacksons. He knew that I had, many years before, received a great deal of talented plastic surgery from that marvellous Scottish pioneer in this field, Sir Archibald McIndoe, famous for his 'guinea pigs', the Battle of Britain pilots, burned and hurt in action. Alex thought that might give us enough common ground to be able to discuss making a film about David. (In fact, I had been through a number of operations on my face to recover my sight, having been blinded. The scarring had been removed by this renowned Scot-with-a-scalpel, who then replaced it with skin taken from 'donor sites' on my buttocks, softer skin and less hairiness. McIndoe's parting comment to me, all those years ago, was that I would be able to tell people that they were listening to a man 'who literally speaks through a hole in his bum.') I had my doubts about this anecdote being totally persuasive for Ian Jackson. But I did, most fervently, believe that it was time for a better understanding of the facially deformed, a better break for those who became the subject of humiliating stares and comments. I agreed to ring the Jacksons.

In the end, that phone call lasted more than two hours – during which time I watched my whole family troop out to the beach, and, hours later, come back! – because I was so fascinated talking to Marjorie. She gave me Ian's work number and I had a briefer but no less absorbing talk with him. We were agreed to make a film about this remarkable child and this just as remarkable man, and his family. I had offered them, as I do with everybody in *The Visit* programmes, the right to view the material first and the thought that it was my intention (this was to be the first series of programmes) always to treat our participants more as partners. I also told him that it was time a documentary raised levels of awareness, dispelled levels of prejudice, about deformity. He and Marjorie were fascinating about the effect it has on a whole family, the almost brutal changes it can bring about in personality, caused by the sufferer literally shrinking from contact with the outside world. Under his helpful eye, there was, in Cellardyke, Fife, a remarkable charity, The Disfigurement Guidance Centre, run by an even more remarkable woman, Doreen Trust, and her husband Peter. Doreen is herself facially disfigured by a 'port wine stain', but such is her confidence and lovely personality that for those of us who admire her it becomes virtually invisible. Her centre offers guidance and help to people and families having to cope with the traumas of disfigurement; what doctors to see, what cosmetics can be used, what surgery might be useful (such as the amazing tunable dye laser so recently brought into use in this country).

When I returned to Glasgow I made plans to film, Alex was delighted. At that time Jan was drafted in to join us, quite specifically, I was told by our boss at the time, Neil Fraser, because she had considerable tact and charm and was particularly good in family situations. He had clearly seen the way the series was developing and he couldn't have been more right about Jan.

Little did I think that we were starting on a road that would lead, in the end, to a total of five documentaries being made about this amazing story. And, as wherever I go quite without exception, I'm always asked when I'm going to bring another 'progress report' on David to the screen, I have the feeling there will be more. So far, more than 30 million viewers, in total, have watched and reacted to the story, many more have seen it around the world – it has been the most syndicated of all *The Visit* films and may have earned back for the BBC many times the cost of making the films.

We shot the first film in Spain and Minnesota and Glasgow. Then we tried to find some kind of library footage of the Campa Indians, in order to show what kind of tribe, what kind of life might have belonged to David. Marjorie was at that time struggling with what seemed like an army of civil servants and bureaucrats to establish an identity for David and protect his future. They had decided they wanted to adopt him. He faced many more years of surgery: when we first met him at the age of eight, he had already undergone more than fifty operations. He was truly a miracle of surgical skill, but also a unique demonstration of parental love and, as well, as an example of young courage. He was athletic, even mischievous, hugely likable, adored by his 'brother' and 'sisters', who spent hours sitting with him in hospital and while recovering from the amazing operations he undertook with such fortitude. Marjorie told me: 'You could film that background material in the jungle itself, I'm sure one can get there – I'd come with you, I'm desperate to see if I can find any formal records for David which will enable us to adopt him and certainly protect him from the United States Immigration authorities. At the moment he's literally an illegal alien and they only hold off deportation because he's still having continuing surgery. Maybe we could get hold of a birth certificate – without that I don't see how we can adopt him.' I reflected gloomily that the odds against a birth certificate having been issued for the tiny baby of a Campa Indian family, part of a wandering Amazonian tribe, were pretty long.

We went back to Neil Fraser and Pat Chalmers, we needed not only their goodwill, but money to finance a trip that had certainly never been envisaged when the programmes were first commissioned. They were marvellous, authorised an extra programme, found the money – not quite enough, but then there never is quite enough money for BBC programmes, and wished us well.

We all travelled to the jungle: light planes across the Andes, dug-out canoes down the river. We had an interpreter, the priest attached to the mission where David had been delivered and where the nuns still remembered him well. We had been to the hospital and the convent headquarters in Lima, found records but still no birth certificate. The Campa Indians moved a lot. Our priest/interpreter thought he remembered the case of the little baby who lost his face. But finding the family would be a needle in a haystack task, quite impossible. We set out to try anyway, sleeping rough, well-zipped in our sleeping-bags at night against the most amazing vampire bats – who probably wouldn't have harmed us but nobody was prepared to take the chance.

And we found the family, astonishingly and miraculously. They were wonderful, simple, dignified and quite unfazed by the presence of a television crew in the middle of the jungle on the banks of a tributary of the Amazon. David had been loved, not abandoned, they cared enough to try to save him. They looked at all the photographs that Marjorie carried with her; they said that he was better off with her. They said it with love, choosing the best chances for the boy. They were a large family, David's father, mother, and seven, maybe eight, brothers and sisters, some perhaps married, one at least pregnant – as was his mother.

Back in the mission, the priest burrowed among mildewed records. David had been baptised, there was a certificate. The needle in the haystack had been found. The priest said it was God's work, I'm inclined to believe him. In Lima we sought the help of the splendid BBC local correspondent there, Elli Griffis de Zuniga, and she arranged for Marjorie to meet the wife of the country's president, who in turn promised to help. That was the second programme and everything looked fine.

We actually won an award for the films but all of us wanted, as our real reward, only to learn that David was improving – and that the adoption had gone through. But snag after snag came up. The law was changing in Peru and would very shortly debar the Jacksons from adopting under any circumstances. Once Ian turned fifty that would be another huge problem. The Jacksons had enlisted their local senator and he was doing his best but it became obvious that the certificate of adoption would have to be issued in Peru, in the jungle, by a local judge. Nothing else would do.

We decided on another film. By then we were so intertwined in this story that there would never have been any question of us standing back and just filming what happened. We were involved, indeed, I like to think that some of it would never have happened without us, I'm sure of it in fact. And if that doesn't say much for stand-your-distance documentary making, then that's not the kind I'm interested in. John

Pettman went with a crew to Peru, then, with Elli and a specialist adoption lawyer, Norma Calderon, they drove, through flood, mountain passes, steaming jungle to the tiny town of Satipo. We were in Minnesota with the Jacksons and another film crew. Time was running out exactly as it always does in the best thrillers. With only twelve hours to go we got the phone call from Elli and Ian was told that the adoption had been made final. At the party, which David thought had been called solely for his aunt's visit, Ian was able to tell all the relatives who had flown in from around the world, that he was no longer David Lopez – he was David Jackson. That's where we ended that film, but not the story.

The United States Immigration service have a very special capacity for putting fences in people's way. The Jacksons still couldn't get David a 'green' card which would allow him not only to stay in the States but to leave (on trips to Glasgow for instance) and come back. Glasgow wanted to honour David and his family by giving David the city's Loving Cup, a quite remarkable gesture for this small courageous boy. He was by now fourteen, attending the local high school, a boy with many friends, and a million admirers round the world. His step-sisters, Linda and Susan had grown up and left home, Linda was married, and Sarah was about to go away to college, as was Andrew his big brother. He was going through the traumas of adolescence. He was still a delight to know. When we filmed this, most recent, programme he picked the where and the when for an interview – on a motorised golf buggy on the local course. The Lady Provost of Glasgow Mrs Susan Baird, presented him with his Loving Cup in a moving ceremony in Rochester. She had flown out with it, complete with her official chain-bearer, because the immigration laws prevented him going to Glasgow.

Since then he has had more operations, a veteran of more than seventy. He looks better every time. Ian and Marjorie have moved to a new home outside Detroit and Ian is now Medical Director of the Institute for Craniofacial and Reconstructive Surgery, which is affiliated with the Providence hospital but, importantly, is also part of the Daughters of Charity

161

National Health System. This allows him to do more charity work. David is now at the local senior school, has made more friends. His story, and his family, have done more than that. Between them they've changed attitudes (Marjorie has had hundreds of moving letters, still receives them); they've taught the rest of us how to deal with facial deformity. How not to take away the dignity and the identity of those who have, for one reason or another, been punished enough when it comes to the way we look.

David is reaching for manhood now, soon he may have to choose a path for himself in the world. He is aware of his beginnings (he's seen all the documentaries) and Ian and Marjorie have often wondered whether he would ever want to go back to the Amazon basin where he was born, to see his roots. Only David can really answer that. Will we be able to ask him, on film, in *The Visit*? He must answer that too but, for the sake of all those admiring and loving people who ask about him nearly every day, I hope the answer will be yes, perhaps when he's leaving college – and the world is truly ahead of him.

A final note

We talked to Marjorie, finished these last chapters, while making the next five films in *The Visit* series. Thus, all three of us – Alex, Jan and myself – spent a week learning how to 'talk' – pretty basically – in British Sign Language, in order to film a moving documentary about the crossroads ahead of two teenage deaf girls. Now, we use it amongst ourselves. It is a fascinating and beautiful language in its own right, part of a deep and worthwhile culture, the culture of the deaf. We learned, too, just what it takes to train the officers and men who so coolly tackle the job of bomb disposal, and we followed them into the 'front line' in Northern Ireland.

And in South America, in Columbia, there's a man who is little short of a saint, rescuing children from gutters, rubbish dumps, even the sewers. But that's another story ... that's another *Visit*.

ACKNOWLEDGEMENTS

Jan Riddell, as always, has tirelessly researched, and talked again to our *Visit* families. Alex McCall remained calm and supportive throughout the hysterical process of writing this book, under pressure, while filming more *Visit* stories. All our friends and colleagues, both in production and among the film crews and in the editing rooms have been more than patient. And if they haven't been mentioned, then I'm sorry and I know they'll understand. And if they have, and they don't like it, I know they'll understand that too....

D.W.

PICTURE CREDITS